Crucible is published quarterly by Hymns Ancient & Modern Ltd.
Registered Charity No. 270060

This publication is in collaboration with the Church of England's
Division of Mission and Public Affairs; the William Temple Foundation.

Editorial board
Stephen Platten, Edward Cardale, Kate Pearson, Elaine Graham,
Malcolm Brown, Chris Swift, Carol Wardman,
Matt Bullimore, James Woodward, Peter Scott, Simon Cuff, Jenny
Leith (Reviews Editor) and Anna Lawrence (Managing Editor).

Correspondence and articles
Correspondence and articles for submission should be sent to Anna
Lawrence at Hymns Ancient and Modern, anna@hymnsam.co.uk.
Articles should be of about 3,000 words.

Subscriptions
(for four copies): individual rate £22; institutions £40;
individual international £40; institutional international £50;
Single copies cost £7.
All prices included postage and packing. Cheques should
be made payable to Crucible, and sent to: Crucible subscriptions,
Subscription Manager, 13a Hellesdon Park Road, Norwich NR6 5DR.

Tel: 01603 785 910   Fax: 01603 624483.
crucible@hymnsam.co.uk

Direct Debit forms available from the same address

ISSN 0011-2100
ISBN 978-0-334-03163-5

Editorial

Graham James   3

Articles

Perceiving the Divine in Beauty   6
Tim Weatherstone

Being "Purpose-led": Reflections for the   15
Church from Working with Business
Charles Wookey

Teaching Christian Ethics - Then and Now   24
Michael J Leyden

Brave New World:
Are We Amusing Ourselves to Death?   34
Graham James and Jan McFarlane

Forum

Church and Kingdom   44
Stephen Platten

Reviews

Andrew Hayes, Tom Mumford, Peter Leith,   52
Rachel Deigh, Edward Cardale

Editorial

GRAHAM JAMES

Among the sectors most affected by changes in consumer spending as a result of Covid-19 has been the cosmetics industry. In the United Kingdom, sales are normally around £2.5 billion a year, but who needs expensive lipstick and make-up when wearing a facemask? Estimates of a reduction in sales approaching 70% are tempered a little by increased expenditure on skincare and hair products. Most people want to appear reasonably well groomed on Zoom.

The plight of the cosmetics industry is unlikely to be one which will lead to episcopal tweets of concern or cause much reflection in learned journals on the effects of the pandemic. It's worth remembering, though, that the glamorous assistants in beauty departments on the high street are, like many who work in this sector, mostly female and very modestly remunerated. The closure of 124 Debenhams stores has had a devastating impact on them.

I only became aware of this issue as a result of guest editing this copy of Crucible. While liaising with Tim Weatherstone about his article on beauty I saw "the beauty industry" referred to in a national newspaper. Increasingly the world of cosmetics is called the beauty industry, and its practitioners are beauticians. There could be no better illustration of the way that the concept of beauty has become a very limited one indeed in Western society.

Our disregard for beauty in theological and ethical discussions is, as Tim Weatherstone seeks to illustrate, mistaken, especially when beauty is no longer dismissed by some scientists and mathematicians as simply a subjective feeling unrelated to real knowledge. As Weatherstone points out, it was not only logical positivists who once thought beauty unimportant and devoid of significance. Karl Barth did so too, and he does not seem much like a natural ally of A.J Ayer. One of the most profound ethical challenges we face is to see beauty in those people and places whom many in our society dismiss as unfruitful or unsustainable.

Editorial

This edition of *Crucible* was not planned with any theme in mind. Intriguingly though, in his article, Charles Wookey, the CEO of *Blueprint for Business*, says that businesses need to attend to the reality that their organizations "form or deform people by the quality of relationships they create". In other words businesses make the world more beautiful when they attend to their social purpose. This frequently also better serves the generation of goods and services, and thus profits. Wookey concludes his article by quoting Gerard Manley Hopkins' reflection that "Christ plays in ten thousand places, lovely in limbs and lovely in eyes not his", sentiments the author describes as "beautiful".

It was assuredly not beautiful when the Church of England decided to remove ethics entirely from the syllabus of theological education for those training for ordination. Michael Leyden's article reflects upon this almost unimaginable turn of events in 1959, which continued for the first half of that seminal decade in the last century, the sixties. Ethics, and especially personal ethics, were scarcely irrelevant then. As Michael Leyden traces, however, much good did come from the eventual reintroduction of ethics into the theological training curriculum and the efforts to make sure it was taught well and creatively. The Society for the Study of Christian Ethics owes its origin to this revival of interest. A multi-disciplinary approach in teaching ethics is now normative. Leyden is not alone in wanting to wrench an understanding of ethics away from being almost wholly concerned with issues and hard cases. "Christian ethics" he says "is bigger than crises". Instead it is about "how to live well" by creating "theologically textured space within everyday life" shaped and moulded by liturgy, Word and sacrament, materials which "have significant moral value: they describe creaturely reality and God's vision for human flourishing in Christ". The expansiveness of this vision of Christian ethics at the heart of discipleship has a beauty about it too. It sees the Christian life as one lived with a profound seamlessness in relation to the whole of the created order.

The inhabitants of New London in Aldous Huxley's *Brave New World* are beautiful, secure and free from diseases and worries. No pandemic for them. Swallowing their Soma pills whenever the slightest anxiety strikes ensures their well-being is immediately restored. As Jan McFarlane and I explore in our joint article the emptiness of this world free from pain and suffering is evident. Much of what is commonly assumed to be a beautiful life turns out not to be so beautiful after all. That was the conviction of Neil Postman, the American scholar who wrote Amusing Ourselves to Death as long ago as 1986. He was sure Huxley's vision was coming about, and that Western society was entertaining itself to death, drowning in a swelling tide of trivialisation. He had no remedy to offer, although he was captivated by the way ancient Israel eschewed images and believed God "was to exist in the Word, and through the Word". But are we amusing ourselves to death, as Postman suggested, or does the Word made flesh challenge both his assumption and the response of Christians to our predicament?

Perhaps there are some threads between these disparate offerings, after all. At present our world seems very disconnected and divided, increasingly deaf to reason as well as religion. The makers of the recent series of Brave New World for television found no place in their narrative for Huxley's cult of Henry Ford. Ford ("Our Ford" to replace "Our Lord") is a messianic figure in the original Brave New World. But the complexity of Huxley's vision had to be simplified and his subtleties ironed out in an age of unreason as well as irreligion. In our era of fake news and conspiracy theories the very currency of debate is debased. So it may be an encouragement that articles commissioned independently for Crucible do interweave, more than I expected, an indication that seeing the world and the ethical task through a Christian lens may lend some beauty to our observation in difficult times.

Graham James was Bishop of Norwich from 1999 to 2019.

Perceiving the Divine in Beauty

Tim Weatherstone

Introduction

Some years ago, I was asked to lead a seminar with a group of church-based youth leaders. Age, church tradition and background separated us, and they were suspicious from the start that they would have nothing to learn from me. I asked them to suspend judgement while I offered some autobiographical details. In order to make a connection I also proffered some objects of art, things of beauty for them to ponder, but these did not prove to be an inducement to listen. The shutters came down and stayed down.

I did not blame them. I would have been much like them myself at their age. This minor incident indicates both how we are liable to fail to learn much from those from whom we are different and also how quickly beauty can be dismissed as something intrinsically worthwhile or interesting, including among Christian audiences. Our refusal to engage with beauty as part of a Christian ethic also has consequences. I have come to believe that a refusal to engage in the quest for beauty underlies a lot of our rejection of each other or of God's creation and fuels our incapacity to love one another.

Recent studies in science demonstrate that beauty matters and is not simply subjective. Further, a desire to seek beauty where we may have previously refused to do so is a potential source of unity. Beauty has the capacity to achieve this without any dilution in personal integrity, and without compromise, which is why it can be of particular value in community building. Such an apprehension of beauty may thus become a motivating ethic, and a tool, in our search for true unity. This would be a benefit in any common endeavour, but perhaps especially so in building our unity in Christ.

Beauty as Challenge

The first decades of my working life were spent first in chemistry and then as a computer programmer. If I thought of it at all, I dismissed the significance of beauty, and the arts meant little to me. Almost 20 years ago I was in London with time on my hands and paid a short visit to the National Gallery. My scientific training had made me fearful of capitulating to any sense of the aesthetic: it was a distraction from rationality and amounted to daydreaming, making one unproductive. Yet two decades ago I was about to enter an entirely new phase of life and work and felt I should be more open-minded about the arts.

What happened that day in the National Gallery was both unexpected and transformative. I was hit by the extraordinary beauty of what I had seen. Now I felt I had to pursue this Cause of Beauty. This transformation also re-interpreted my past. I had been a computer programmer for well over a decade. My code was of an obscure kind and rarely even seen by anybody. I always knew my code had to be well written, but I also required it to be elegant. Managers may have had little interest, yet my colleagues and I knew that code was about something more than function. I now understood that the coding process was driven by beauty. As I worked through this transformation, I realised I had encountered this sense of the beautiful before.

I also knew that I had been found out. All my life I had told myself to reject such evaluations as being wasteful; they leached productivity out of you. I was wrong: beautiful computer code was demonstrably more effective and easier to maintain. I knew this from years of hard graft, night and day, in our dark coding dungeons. (Programmers, so managers seemed to think, should not be allowed desks too close to windows and were best housed in dark spaces).

Commentary on Beauty

Beauty, we are told, is 'in the eye of the beholder'. Immanuel Kant tells us:

> In order to decide whether or not something is beautiful, we do not relate the representation by means of understanding to the object for cognition, but rather relate it by means of the imagination (perhaps combined with the understanding) to the subject and its feeling of pleasure or displeasure. The judgment of taste is therefore not a cognitive judgment, hence not a logical one, but is

> rather aesthetic, by which is understood one whose determining ground cannot be other than subjective. (Kant, 89)

Hence, according to Kant, something is beautiful because it gives us pleasure; such judgements have to do with our sense of taste. In his understanding, they are subjective and illogical.

Kant is not alone. AJ Ayer goes further:

> Such aesthetic words as 'beautiful' and 'hideous' are employed, as ethical words are employed, not to make statements of fact, but simply to express certain feelings and evoke a certain response. It follows, as in ethics, that there is no sense in attributing objective validity to aesthetic judgements, and no possibility of arguing about questions of value in aesthetics, but only about questions of fact …. We conclude, therefore, that there is nothing in aesthetics, any more than there is in ethics, to justify the view that it embodies a unique form of knowledge. (Ayer, 118)

Ayer published his most famous work, 'Language, Truth and Logic', in the 1930s. Ayers' biographer Ben Rogers, in attempting to describe the profound impact that small book had upon pre-war analytic philosophy, writes in the introduction to a 2001 edition of the work:

> Nevertheless, the abiding quality of Language, Truth and Logic lies not in its detailed arguments but in something else. This is a book that is, somehow, more than the sum of its parts. (Ayer, xvi)

Rogers goes on to speak of the 'zeal' poured into Ayer's writing and that he has a 'passion for truth'. Ayer's thesis is that sentences which assert a reality to exist 'beyond the limits of all possible sense experience"are nonsensical. From this it follows that in Ayers' understanding, any talk of 'zeal' or 'passion' must also be without meaning. Yet his biographer states in effect that this is the entire meaning of the book and that its true worth emerges between the words, beyond sense experience. Rogers declares, against his very subject, that value-laden qualitative considerations exceed in importance apparently quantitative and measurable attributes of our knowledge. Zeal and passion, beauty and further aesthetic considerations thus become 'facts'; facts of a different kind, yet components within our knowledge base of anything.

Theologians too have been unfriendly to beauty. Karl Barth

claimed that beauty was not a 'primary motif in our understanding of the whole being of God' (Barth, 652). I had plainly been in distinguished company, yet I now knew that this was wrong: beauty was not 'merely' subjective. It was something real and outside myself; beauty contributed uniquely to knowledge. I remembered where I had seen beauty before.

Beauty as Science

My drive to create what I and my colleagues revelled in as 'beautiful code', was borne not of some passing fad or scanty acquaintance, but an almost unreasonable fixation upon the task of self-improvement.

Years earlier I had trained as a chemist. I had been impressed by those who could sense through graphs, gauges and other machine outputs, that something of real beauty was being driven to happen in a test tube or reactor.

Fast forward to more recent times when I was pursuing further studies. I went back to my earlier discipline (the chemistry and not the computing) and caught-up with current practice and results. Time and again, in apparently dry, detailed, complex reports in research papers, beauty mattered. In the mid-2010s researchers of long standing were making judgements about where and how to pursue future avenues of research, based upon perceptions of beauty.

Such judgements are value judgements. They cannot be measured: one cannot have some quantity of beauty, some 'bits' of beauty. Such are qualitative judgements, not quantitative. They are qualitative but also objective; substantive, rational and not illogical. They are value judgements which drive research in one of the 'hard' sciences. This is not merely my opinion.

An American Chemistry Professor, Peter Walhout, affirms the "reliability of beauty":

> An aesthetic intersubjective acceptance based on harmony with existing scientific understanding also plays a role, and beauty is a reliable guide for reason in the search for new scientific truths. (Walhout, 774)

The British mathematical physicist and philosopher of science Sir Roger Penrose recently remarked:

Perceiving the Divine in Beauty

> It might be the case that we are entering a new phase of basic research into fundamental physics, where requirements of mathematical consistency become paramount, and in those situations where such requirements [...] prove insufficient, additional criteria of mathematical elegance and simplicity must be invoked. While it may seem unscientific to appeal to such aesthetic desiderata in a fully objective search for the physical principles underlying the workings of the universe, it is remarkable how fruitful - indeed essential - such aesthetic judgements seem to have frequently proved to be. (Penrose, 2)

Many will be aware of mathematicians speaking of the beauty of certain equations, yet what we have here is more than that. What Penrose and Walhout imply is that this new tool of 'aesthetic judgement', when wielded by seasoned practitioners, can advance the sum total of human knowledge. Beauty perceived thus, is indicative of a 'something' that is outside of Self.

Once we have understood that beauty has a value in and of itself, separate (though not divorced) from personal aesthetic considerations, we may re-visit what we already find beautiful in the physical world and enrich that 'perception event' with what we have learned.

The Christ of Beauty

Discernment of beauty stretches across fields of human knowledge but nowhere is it more prevalent in general perception than in nature and particularly in our response to the countryside. This has inspired poets across the generations.

> 'Twas late in my long journey, when I had clomb to where
> the path was narrowing and the company few,
> a glow of childlike wonder enthral'd me, as if my sense
> had come to a new birth purified, my mind enrapt
> re-awakening to a fresh initiation of life;
> with like surprise of joy as any man may know
> who rambling wide hath turn'd, resting on some hill-top
> to view the plain he has left, and see'th it now out-spredd
> mapp'd at his feet, a landscape so by beauty estranged
> he scarce wil ken familiar haunts, nor his own home,
> maybe, where far it lieth, small as a faded thought.' (Bridges, 2)

So wrote Robert Bridges. He was the Poet Laureate in the early part of last century and the writer and translator of well-known hymns. What is perhaps less well known is that he was also a scientist, a doctor by training. The journey he was speaking of above in 1929, was his life's journey since he died a year later at the age of 85. The beauty in the landscape which he saw in a childlike way gave rise to a fresh initiation into life, just as it was coming to an end. Bridges was also a devout Christian. Elsewhere in the same work he muses about whether bees are driven to their familiar corporate ways through some 'organic socialism' that is likewise part of the substance that they themselves are composed of, and goes on to describe how 'mathematic formulae pregnant of truth' (Bridges, 49-50) point the way to the Divine. Again, Bridges is speaking of beauty as something fundamental in the fabric of the Universe.

Our exegesis of Genesis 1 and 2 may have hampered our ability to perceive purpose in Creation. Commentators have long suggested that the destruction of the Garden of Eden in the Fall rendered discernment of the Divine in the physical world fraught with all manner of dangers from the political to the syncretistic. Western Christianity, reflecting Enlightenment concepts of order, came to see the creation through a 'glass darkly' (1 Corinthians 13.12) so thoroughly that the profound and immediate witness of the Holy Spirit in creation was unsighted (Colossians 1.27, Galatians 3.2,3). Paradoxically, this replaced the offering of an intimate and enabling Divine relationship, with a potentially blinding pelagianism. David Tsumara argues that we may have become too easily dazzled by ancient creation myths, believing them, sometimes mistakenly, to be closely linked to the Genesis accounts (Tsumura 1989, 156-159). Thus distracted, we fail to grasp the unique revelation contained in Genesis, namely that in Creation God transformed that which was unproductive into something functional rather than perfect, and that God's purpose in Creation persists (Tsumura 1989, 156).

In this short essay I have sought to illustrate that our perception of beauty, both in the arts and in the natural world, as well as in these strangely 'unseen"ways in the sciences, is part of the Divine purpose of self-revelation in Creation (Weatherstone, 64). We read in Psalm 27.4 of a desire to contemplate the beauty, delightfulness and splendour of God, eternally. Psalm 96.6 too speaks of the 'strength and beauty' of God.

It is well-known that ancient Hebrew is a language whose referents are those which induce a physical response; the text is always inviting us to respond in action. In translation several Hebrew words are rendered as 'beauty' or one of its cognates. We like one-to-one correspondence in language and seek an exact equivalence in words to that which we see or sense. Yet the beauty I am speaking of is in respect of things unseen; what is it we are sensing? We cannot see the beautiful molecule of which the chemist speaks. We may not be able to understand what it is that a practitioner perceives as beautiful about their mathematical equation or their computer code. Indeed, we cannot always understand why the painting or the landscape we describe as being beautiful, is precisely that. What is it we are responding to? Is it a sense of grandeur or splendour, as spoken of in the Psalms above? Is it a 'something' that overwhelms us with its intelligence and coherence of form? Surely it is always a 'something' more than simply being 'pretty'?

Consider a word such as 'shape': a musician may 'shape' a phrase and so may an author. So too may an engineer 'shape' a body-panel. Yet the craft exercised in the action and the discernment of the final solution, requires a similar perception of the end each is seeking. The attribute of 'shape' may help us to comprehend the 'something' which constitutes beauty. It is in the action of responding to a shape or surface whether concrete or in the "mind's eye", that we acknowledge inherent beauty (Weatherstone, 157-162). While this requires no act of faith but is part of the nature of insight, I believe such a perception of beauty is of the God who is present but unseen. The beauty of the 'shape' of the mathematics or physics or chemistry, or of coding logic, or any other such perceived surface, is unseen but points to the Unseen who formed it.

Beauty as Ethic in Unity

The way in which scientists and others now speak of beauty may be interesting and intriguing, but if this quest for beauty underlies our search for truth and meaning it has ethical consequences for our daily behaviour an interaction, and our quest for unity with others.

I began this article by recalling a gathering where I had a gap to bridge with my audience, which I failed to do. In my own faith journey, I had been like those youth leaders who doubted that those from traditions of the Church they did not inhabit, who seemed very "other", had much useful to offer them. Now I was such an 'other' but what I was wanting for my audience was to experience that same journey God had dragged me through, a journey into each other, to see beauty in unexpected and hidden places.

Today I minister in small rural parishes, among communities which are sometimes told they are unsustainable. Contemporary society (including the contemporary Church) does not perceive much beauty in small, frequently elderly groups of people faithfully serving those among whom they live. Yet many of my colleagues and parishioners have taught me much about beauty through the witness of their long lives of service, not least by their refusal to deny the beauty of those others in our communities they are called to serve. They perceive beauty in the people, places and communities around them very readily and connect that beauty naturally with God. They are not wrong to do so, as I have discovered.

The consequence of all this is that I have been taught that I should think less of my taste and my response in any discernment of beauty. Instead, I should endeavour to perceive Christ in the most unexpected places, invisibly, quietly and in the most - perhaps - unlikely people. I may feel unsympathetic towards someone as I prepare to meet them, yet once I do so Christ frequently tells me a different story. It isn't my story, but the story of Christ in them, in their passions and loves and desires. It is the beauty of Christ in them.

It's possible to fail to discern this. Worse would be to refuse wilfully to see beauty in places, things, events and people, where those very people do so in their own places and circumstances. Choosing not to do so now seems to me to constitute 'opposing the ordinance of God'.

Thus, to perceive and acknowledge beauty where I would once have refused to discern it, becomes a bridge, an ethic, to share and build community with those I live and work alongside. This is not some superficial 'warm feeling'; it is partaking in the very heartbeat of the Universe; it is the experience of Unity in Christ, the Χριστὸς Παντοκράτωρ; the unity He demands of us, towards and with those among whom He places us.

The Revd Dr Tim Weatherstone is Rector of the Barnham Broom and Upper Yare benefice in the Diocese of Norwich.

Questions for Discussion

1. Towards the end of the Epistle to the Romans, Paul urges unity to prevail beyond questions of food and differences over the liturgical calendar. If these were the 'deal-breaker' issues then, what does that say about the issues that divide Christian communities today?

2. Given that the gift of Beauty proceeds from the Creator and indicates the Divine Presence, how might this insight revise individual attitudes towards different forms of worship, or indeed various fields of endeavour?

3. How does an aesthetic appreciation (as seen for example in the "art for art's sake" movement of the 19th century) differ from beauty with a divine foundation as discussed above?

References

Ayer, A.J., 1936. *Language, Truth and Logic*. Reprint 2001. London: Penguin Books Ltd.

Barth, K., 1957. *Church Dogmatics, Volume 2: The Doctrine of God*, Part 1. Translated from German by T.H.L Parker, W.B. Johnston, H. Knight, J.L.M. Hair. Edinburgh, T. & T. Clark.

Bridges, Robert, 1929. *The Testament of Beauty*. Oxford: The Clarendon Press.

Kant, I., 2000. *Critique of the Power of Judgment*. Paul Guyer (ed.). Translated from German by P., Guyer and E., Matthews. Cambridge: CUP.

Penrose, Roger, 2016. *Fashion, Faith and Fantasy in the New Physics of the Universe*. Princeton: Princeton University Press.

Tsumura, David, 1989. *The Earth and the Waters in Genesis 1 and 2: A Linguistic Investigation*. Sheffield: JSOT Press.

Walhout, P.K., 2009. *The Beautiful and the Sublime in Natural Science*. Zygon, 44(4). pp. 757-776.

Weatherstone, Timothy, 2017. *Reconstructing Wonder: Chemistry Informing a Natural Theology*. Frankfurt am Main: Peter Lang Edition.

— Being "Purpose-led" —

Reflections for the Church from Working with Business

CHARLES WOOKEY

In the summer of 1995 eight senior business leaders spent a weekend at the Benedictine monastery of Worth Abbey in Sussex. They were invited to explore with a group of monks what a business and a monastery may have in common. They came intrigued by the thought that the Rule of St Benedict had been continuously guiding monastic life for 1400 years. Maybe there was something to learn here that might help their businesses to be sustainable in the long-term. The only pre-read was the Rule.

The CEO of a hotel group had read closely the chapter in the Rule about hospitality – the importance of treating any guest to the monastery as Christ. He was very moved by this, and then reflected on the quality of genuine care and consideration for guests which the best hotels showed, and which could not be faked. Towards the end of the closing session another business leader said, "I run an organisation but what I've realised over this weekend is that it's also a community". The Abbot of Worth Stephen Ortiger then replied "Thank you. We live in a community and what I have learned over this weekend is there is something to be said for being organised!"

In 1960 shortly before his death one of the founders of Hewlett Packard, David Packard gave a speech reflecting on his company. He said:

> "...a group of people get together and exists as an institution we call a company so they are able to accomplish something collectively which they could not do separately. They are able to do something worthwhile – they make a contribution to society (a phrase which sounds trite but is fundamental)". (Miller J,50)

In a different plane the Church has a similar rationale. Jesus called his disciples friends, and if anyone wanted to be one of them, they had to accept and join his other friends - they were committing to follow him as a band, becoming something together that they could not accomplish alone.

How the purpose of any shared endeavour is characterised, and how people are thought about, shapes what happens. In recent decades we have seen the consequences in business when narrow and reductive ideas about purpose and people take hold. In this article we will explore how a charity formed after the great financial crisis is helping to challenge these dominant ideas and support businesses to inhabit a more creative and generative sense of their role as social organisations. We will then look to see what parallels there may be in the world of the institutional Church, which is currently suffering its own distinctive travails, and where an exchange of insights may yield some hopeful pointers.

Blueprint for Better Business was established as a charity in 2014 but its origins in fact go back to a seminar of City leaders held at Schroder's bank in 2009, reflecting on what had gone wrong. Pope Benedict had just published his Encyclical on Catholic Social Thought *Caritas in Veritate*, and Brian Griffiths, Vice chair of Goldman Sachs rang the Archbishop of Westminster's office. "This contains by far the best ethical critique of what has gone wrong. You should use this to engage with City leaders." The seminars drew on the insights in the encyclical to focus on business culture and the breakdown of trust. But in the following months the City leaders attention gradually drifted to how to restore reputation. A City values project in 2010 started with the aim "to ensure the city retains its premier status as a financial centre". As several of us pointed out at the time, this aim seemed transparently self-serving. The logic appeared to be - "We need you to trust us so we can make more money out of you in future." A better starting point, some of us suggested, would be to ask a more fundamental question: What is the point of the financial services industry? Who does it exist to serve? And what then needs to change if it is to do a better job of providing that service?

The group of business leaders and others who got together to found Blueprint in 2012 became convinced that asking what the point of a business is – that is, why does it exist at all, was a necessary and timely one. This is because the dominant answer provided by Milton Friedman 50 years go – which had shaped much of business life and practice in the UK and US since then – was at the core of many of the problems. Friedman's answer was a very different one from David Packard. He said that the purpose of business was to increase its profits within law and ethical custom. This is neither a law of physics nor what the civil law demands, at least in the UK. It is, in fact, just an idea – and a very powerful one - especially when combined with the thought that people are assumed to be atomised individuals motivated by money, status and power. Put these together, align incentives well, the maths all works and people seeking no more than their own self-interest will behave in a way that enables a company to maximise its profits.

These two ideas have helped shape the business world, and that world became deeply scarred by a double disconnect. The first is between business and society, and it arose when the narrow pursuit of profit maximisation allowed companies to think of themselves as apart from society. It legitimised, at its worst, their failure to respect the dignity of people, through unjust distribution of pay and benefits, exploiting communities, heedless damage to the environment, opposing necessary regulation and failing to pay tax.

This has become a familiar critique. But there is a second and deeper disconnect less often noticed by people in business. It is in the human heart. We are not merely individuals motivated by self-interest, as both the wisdom traditions and empirical disciplines such as neuroscience and positive psychology increasingly recognise. They point instead to three other aspects of what it means to be human. First, we are fundamentally relational as well as individual, with a desire to cooperate and belong, to care for others and be cared for. Second, we seek meaning and want to contribute to the world through our lives and our work. Third, we seek through work ideally to grow, gain autonomy and in some way to realise our potential. When work frustrates these impulses, people live divided lives. They leave part of themselves at the virtual office door. The human costs are evident in low employee morale and mental health problems. The business costs include reduced commitment, productivity and innovation, and increased regulatory and reputational risk from breaches and scandals.

Blueprint was established to achieve real change in the relationship between business and society by challenging how businesses think about *both* purpose and people. Part of the shift was for businesses to recognize that they mostly can and should have a reason for being which benefits society – reflected in what a business says, what it does

Being "Purpose-led"

and how it does it. Profit is vital, but as one outcome, not the purpose. The other is that a business needs to recognize that it is a social organization, and to care about people whether they are employees, customers, suppliers or the communities on which the business depends. There is a latent capacity for people to commit – providing discretionary effort - which comes from feeling they are 'valued members of a winning team on a worthwhile mission.' – to quote one CEO It is better for business, better for society and better for people. It is just not easy to achieve.

Why? Because it is always both an organisational and a personal challenge, and also a systemic one. Organisationally it requires creating a compelling narrative and operating model which links the purpose to the strategy and the outcomes from the strategy back to the purpose. It also depends crucially on how people behave and fostering a culture where each person is seen as a "someone not a something". This is a personal challenge because we all have choices in how we decide to show up at work, what commitment we are willing to make to others, and whether we are ourselves willing to challenge and change our own assumptions and behaviour, and especially the frame of mind we bring to work.

This question of mindset is the fundamental one. In *The Future We Choose*, her book on negotiating the 2015 Paris Climate agreement, Christiana Figueres writes

> "..if you do not control the complex landscape of a challenge (and you rarely do), the most powerful thing you can do is to change how you behave in that landscape, using yourself as a catalyst for overall change. All too often in the face of task, we move quickly to "doing "without first reflecting on "being" – what we personally bring to the task, as well as what others might. *And the most important thing we can bring is our state of mind.*" (Figueres, p 49 emphasis added)

When he was running Marks & Spencer in its heyday Marcus Seiff was reputedly forensic in his inspection of margins on individual product lines. He would as one may expect be very curious when margins were too low. But he was equally curious when he thought margins were too high – was M & S charging its customers too much or paying its suppliers too little? He had an instinctive sense of fairness where customers and suppliers would feel they were being well served. He wanted relationships not transactions, and he also believed that doing so led to a successful long-term business even if it did not maximise short term profits.

Alongside such an organisational mindset what is also needed, and especially now, is an awareness of the systemic dimension. The market never exists in a pure state and is always a social and cultural construct. UN climate change documents have described the change needed today as moving from an economic system optimised for growth and profit to one optimised for human well being and a sustainable ecosystem. Growth and profit are both still needed – but not as ends in themselves but as means to these broader systemic goals. In a world of rising temperature and rising social inequality this overarching narrative - which applies as much to governments and the third sector as well - provides a powerful reinforcement to the logic of business becoming" purpose- led". It is the way business contributes to, rather than obstructs, this vital systemic change which the world needs.

So how may these provocations about purpose and people, with which the business world is now familiar, be applied to wider systemic issues in the Church?

First of all, the Church does not exist for its own sake. Its purpose - its reason for being - is to be a sign and symbol of the reconciliation between God and humanity achieved by the life, death and resurrection of Christ. It carries this mission through history as a community of people gathered together, through what they say, what they do and how they do it.

But even the best foundational purpose can become obscured. When she took over as CEO of the homeless charity Shelter in the late 1980s, Sheila McKechnie found a highly purposeful organisation that had lost its way. "It should be a campaign for the homeless", she said. "But it's become a home for campaigners". She had a major job to change a culture that had become self-serving.

There are many facets to the critique of the churches over the child abuse scandals, and they are both shocking and tragic. But one fundamental aspect is the way in which many - though not all - senior people thought about their duty to the institution. They allowed themselves to think that the Church did exist for its own sake, and their role was to protect the institution rather than to serve the gospel, often unthinkingly putting the good name of the Church ahead of the care of victims and survivors.

A good purpose in business always reveals the gap between the

Being "Purpose-led"

current state and what some future better world which the business can help bring into being. It fosters aspiration and stimulates innovation and creativity about better ways the business can realise that purpose. The Church's true purpose constantly calls the institution to reflect on its role and work and illuminates both its shortcomings and the path ahead. And indeed the most powerful sources of change and renewal from within the Church today are coming from a reappraisal of how best to serve the Gospel. This recognises in the painful exposures of the corruption of power and hypocrisy the true seeds of spiritual freedom in humility, seeking the truth wherever it leads and utter dependence on Christ.

A related aspect of this shift is noted by Christiana Figueres, in the quote above, on the relationship between 'being' and 'doing'. I had the great privilege of being Cardinal Basil Hume's public affairs assistant for 11 years until he died in 1999 aged 75. He would often put his head round the door for a brief chat. I recall him coming into the office after his 70th birthday, and announcing baldly, "I've made a decision. I'm going to be more and do less. Goodbye." He meant it. Fewer lectures, more parish visits, more time in prayer and reflection, less busyness.

He was rare. It seems a risk of both business and church leaders to be action addicted. Charles Handy, the organisational expert once spent a day with the Catholic bishops on their study week. One image he uses in his work is a doughnut – any job has a core element in the middle which circumscribes the things you must do. Then around it and within the outer ring is space for discretionary activities - which you can do if you wish. Working within that outer ring is often the source of energy, renewal and creativity. He reflected afterwards that the trouble with the bishops was their lives are almost all core. By that he meant that the burden of activities and obligations on them was such that they had little time and energy to spend in the penumbra. The culture of the institutional Church exacerbates this tendency by placing too many burdens on the best people. It is not surprising that burnout, depression and stress are common in church leaders.

I recall reading about an American CEO who said there were three key parts to the job. Define reality, say thank you, and get out of the way. Define reality – create the narrative about the purpose and strategy in a way that is compelling and inspiring, so people understand the shared worthwhile endeavour and are inspired to be part of it. Say thank you – spend lots of time finding the good things that are happening and thank those individuals responsible (by the time he retired CEO Douglas Conant had sent 30,000 handwritten thank you cards (Conant, 2)). And get out of the way - appoint good people and then do not micromanage.

One of the many fascinating changes taking place in the business world as a result of Covid is in the internal culture of large organisations that have had to adapt to remote working, which does not lend itself to command and control. The backstory of people's lives is visible through the zoom window, and suddenly the quality of human relationships has become much more important. People have had to be trusted to get on with it, and often they have done so. Less oversight has led to more innovation and creativity, less control to higher trust. Less core, more penumbra.

In some ways, though, the Church can have the opposite problem - not releasing people from too much control but being able to create any sense of a shared endeavour. When I started at the Catholic Bishops' Conference in 2001, I was asked to create an HR function and reorganise the team. The overt contract was a bunch of people committed to the Church working together who did not mind about being paid poorly because they believed in the mission. The hidden psychological contract was rather different. People felt undervalued because they were badly looked after and were highly resistant to any challenge or suggestion of common action. They all just did their own thing and would only do the things they personally cared about. It took time, significantly increased pay and a number of staff changes to create a more professional culture with a genuinely shared sense of collective purpose.

Sr Helen Alford, whose thinking has been instrumental in shaping the work of Blueprint, frequently uses the analogy of friendship to describe the common goods an organisation creates. It is a simple but profound insight for people soaked in the culture of individualism which has done so much to distort and narrow our vision of what is possible. When people become friends, they create something together – the friendship – which is a shared good, and one that only exists because of the commitment both have made. It is real but cannot be cut up or shared out. In the business world today where so much of the value lies in the people who work together, there is increased recognition that the value for society created by the business is far more - and more important – than just returns to investors. The language of "stakeholders" gestures towards this but is still inadequate as it presumes a mindset of competing interests where the question is a fairer distribution of the benefits or sharing of the burdens. What is needed is a richer language to characterise the social friendships which businesses can create and to draw attention to the human reality that businesses form or deform people by the quality of relationships they create, and through which they generate goods and services, and so profits.

When we started Blueprint a number of theologians pointed us to the importance of moving from doing things 'to and for' people to 'with and alongside' them, inviting people into a process of creating shared goods through relationships based on respect for the dignity of people. One implication is the importance of dialogue and the need for true accountability. In different ways this remains a huge challenge both for businesses and the Church. If businesses exist to serve and benefit society and not just make money for shareholders, how do they best hold themselves accountable to society for what they do? How could they innovate to create new forms of dialogue if the law does not require it? If the Church does not exist for its own sake but the sake of humanity, how should the institutional side of the Church hold itself accountable not only in a hierarchal sense but also to the communities it exists to serve?

The Church as an institution exists to point to Christ in whom Christians believe we find the best answer to the question 'What does it mean to be human?' But we also know that:

> "... Christ plays in ten thousand places
> Lovely in limbs and lovely in eyes not his,
> To the Father in the features of men's faces." (Hopkins, 51)

Despite the lack of inclusive language, Hopkins's insight remains beautiful. It may be there are some stirrings in the business world that have something to say to the Church as she is prompted to think in a different way about purpose and people. A renewed and thoughtful dialogue about creating the conditions for human fulfilment would be enriching for both.

Charles Wookey is CEO and co-founder of A Blueprint for Better Business (www.blueprintforbusiness.org), a charity helping businesses to be a force for good. He was previously Assistant for Public Affairs to Cardinal Hume from 1988-1999, and Assistant General Secretary of the Catholic Bishops Conference of England and Wales until 2016.

Questions for discussion

1. "Define reality and get out of the way." This may seem like good advice for church leaders but who defines reality in the Church today, and out of whose way should those people get?

2. As with the business leaders at Worth Abbey, the Rule of St Benedict has proved newly attractive within the Church and well beyond the Church in the past generation. Why is this so, and what may we learn from it about what it says to our common search for human fulfilment?

3. What are the areas of the Rule we are likely to ignore as too uncomfortable?

References

Conant D, 2011, *Secrets of Positive Feedback*, Harvard Business Review

Figueres C and Rivett-Carnac T, 2020, *The Future We Choose*, London, Manilla Press

Hopkins GM, 1953 *Selected Poems and Prose edited by W H Gardner*, London, Penguin

Miller J and Parker L, 2013, *Everybody's Business*, London, Biteback publishing Ltd.

Teaching Christian Ethics

Then and Now

Michael J Leyden

Introduction

It is a very-nearly unbelievable fact that for a brief period in the mid-twentieth century the Church of England stopped teaching ethics and moral reasoning to its ordinands. Between 1959 and 1964 the discipline was dropped from the prescribed syllabus of the General Ordination Exam (GOE), the Church's end-of-training standard since 1921. The reasons for this change are complex, but there is general agreement that the teaching of Christian ethics within theological colleges was not then in good health, reflecting a general paucity of expertise nationally with only a couple of university Chairs and very few lectureships in the field (Harries, 2020; Platten, 2013, 210). Indeed, professional guilds such as the Roman Catholic Association of Teachers of Moral Theology (1968) and The Society for the Study of Christian Ethics (1983) were yet to come into existence. Where ethics and moral reasoning had been taught in theological colleges, it tended towards history and philosophy with little understanding of the pressing issues of the day or, indeed, how deacons and priests might draw upon the material substance of their ministries (word and sacrament) to help parishioners as they wrestled with those issues. The existing college syllabus seemed irrelevant to the questions people were asking and the changing context of ministry.

From the vantage point of 2021, the deletion of ethics from the curriculum is incredible for at least two reasons. The first is the implication that Christian faith had little ethical import, either because the content of the module was remote from the practicalities of life and the daily grind of decisions and actions that people live with, or because those who taught it 'were not properly qualified to teach it' (Harries, 2020) indicating a significant level of triviality. It is even more bizarre when one remembers the contemporary reports produced by the Church of England Board of Social Responsibility: *Sterilization: An Ethical Enquiry* (1962), *Abortion: An Ethical Discussion* (1965), and *Decisions about Life and Death: A Problem of Modern Medicine* (1965). The institutional Church was contributing to conversations its ministers were not prepared for! A second reason we might be incredulous is the pervasiveness of ethical discourse in the Church of England today. We continue to wrestle with the application of truth, forgiveness, and justice in the light of revelations of abuse; to disagree over the meaning of marriage and whether sexual difference is really axiomatic; to wrestle with an ongoing unease about good disagreement, mutual flourishing, and the fragile unity of the church; as well as our corporate struggle for just representation and opportunity for our sisters and brothers from black and minority ethnic backgrounds. To think that less than 60 years ago the tools and skills necessary for navigating these discussions were not taught to the ministers of the Church of England is...odd.

Happily, the suspension from the GOE was short-lived. 'Continuing protests' from some senior clergy and the handful of professional Christian ethicists working in universities, put gentle pressure on the Ordination Candidates Committee to revisit the decision (ACCM, 1974, vii). Though it was recognised that a return to the inadequacies of the previous iteration of the syllabus would be inappropriate, it was also clear that to side-step the disciplines of ethics and moral reasoning would ill-equip ordinands for their futures as parish priests. A more professional approach was needed. What emerged was the publication by the Advisory Council for the Church's Ministry (ACCM) of *A Handbook for Teachers of Christian Ethics in Theological Colleges* in 1964. It was not a comprehensive syllabus, and certainly not a manual or primer. The Chair of the Council described it as 'a preliminary contribution towards the task of discovering a satisfactory syllabus and a method for teaching this subject' (cit. Platten, 2013, 211). The more mature syllabus emerged ten years later and was published as *Teaching Christian Ethics*. It was described by the Working Group that produced it as 'a revision in the light of experience' (ACCM, 1974, vii). In what follows I shall outline some of the themes and contours of that mature syllabus before reflecting on three notable aspects of its approach.

The 1974 Syllabus

The mature GOE syllabus was the product of a working group that met in June 1972, chaired by the Dean of King's College London, Sydney Evans. It comprised a further six lay and ordained people, including teachers from universities and theological colleges, a bishop's adviser, and the Secretary of the Theological Education Committee of the ACCM, Ronald Coppin – 'The very small group of people who seemed to know anything at all about Christian ethics at that time' (Harries cited in Platten, 2013, 212). The final draft 'was worked through at a seminar of theological college teachers together with the working group...in March 1973' (ACCM, 1974, viii). The main focus was as we might expect: 'to help the student, particularly the ordinand, to acquire some kind of moral compass and direction-finder both for his own need in steering his life in a society which has no single ethical or philosophical framework of reference and no less for his work as teacher, preacher, pastor' (1974, 1). It was not that the ordinands were without any moral fibre to begin with, but rather what made the acquisition of these skills necessary was the sharpness of the ethical questions raised by rapid technological advancement in the post-war West – 'thermonuclear weapons, mass media, international transport, the contraceptive pill' – and the view that these developments and their associated moral quandaries were unprecedented. The need for a fresh moral compass was doubtless compounded by the advancement of secularisation and the discombobulating experience of 1960s Church of England Radicalism, which questioned all the usual presumptions of Christian faith and with them the traditional ethical route-markers, all the while trying (but ultimately failing) to advance an alternative (see Brewitt-Taylor, 2018). Ordinands thus found themselves 'in a social context where there [were] other understandings of man [sic.] ...other assumptions about behaviour and responsibility which cause confusion and no little bewilderment' (ACCM, 1974, 2). The syllabus sought to connect Christian faith to the social order in which the Christian life was to be lived and in which moral reason was to be exercised.

Following an introductory section outlining basic concerns, the syllabus contained four distinct foci. The first was the identity of the Christian community and the distinctive materials it uses for constructing meaning. In particular, it called for close attention to the biblical material – 'what is in the bible rather than theories about what is in the bible' (1974, 15) – and the interpretative role of the Christian tradition in forming our moral imaginations. Of the latter, the syllabus suggested either a discussion of key persons and traditions, citing Augustine, Aquinas, Luther, Calvin and Liberation Theology as most worthy of attention, or else for the teacher to 'select themes and questions of special interest' (1974, 40) which could then be explored from a range of perspectives. Both pedagogical approaches will be familiar to Christian ethicists today. The second focus concerned the inherent problems and pitfalls of trying to relate theology to ethical deliberation. There are layers to this discussion, which require attention to the material claims of Christian faith (what we may think of as revelation) and whether or not we may derive the ethical 'ought' from the revelatory 'is'. If revelation is important, how do we extend Christian moral reasoning to speak into a secular world of competing assumptions in ways that address general human concerns? One aspect of this question will be considered in the final section of this essay. An important point highlighted in the syllabus is whether or not 'Christian' ethics is trying to do the same work as secular or non-Christian ethics, and whether it is even possible to think of an overlap – as if 'Christian' ethics might be a species of ethics more generally. To my mind the syllabus does not deal sufficiently with the peculiar claims of Christian doctrine at this point, and so it does not deal effectively with the peculiar worldview that Christianity affords (1974, 80-83; see also Leyden, 2019, 9-28). The third focus was the necessity and challenge of doing Christian moral reasoning in the 'social, political, and economic realms' of a modern secular society (1974, 90). The GOE syllabus laments approaches to Christian ethics that are overly concerned for the personal morality and character of individuals at the expense of society: ethics is not a means of escaping the world in which Christians find themselves, but a tool that helps the faithful to enact Christian virtues within that world. Importantly, this section of the syllabus recognised that Christians have many of the same concerns as their neighbours, and it encouraged some focus on international issues (e.g. war and nationalism), national issues (e.g. justice, race, and politics), industrial and economic issues (e.g. property and employment), and family issues (e.g. sex and sexuality, sounding a positive note on the reception of the Wolfenden Report and the revised Sexual Offences Act 1967 – see ACCM, 1974, 106-07). The final focus within the syllabus was the particularity of moral reasoning in the context of parochial ministry. This section was considerably shorter than the others, but, of course, in the context

Christian Ethics

of mid-twentieth century ministerial training we may imagine it was thought the actual doing of ethics was better suited to the concrete reality of curacy than the classroom. That said, Appendix 4 'Handling a Specific Moral Case' offered a brief overview of the necessary steps towards making a moral judgement and what might be involved in offering considered opinions to those desiring clerical counsel. Each section came with a reading list, reminding us that this was a syllabus overview rather than an ethics primer or textbook.

Like all academic books, *Teaching Christian Ethics* demonstrates the peculiarities of its own time and context. Nevertheless, though the GOE (and its successor from 1978, the General Ministerial Examination) have been obsolete for 30 years, there are worthwhile insights for today.

Teaching Christian Ethics Today

Three aspects of the approach in *Teaching Christian Ethics* I think are noteworthy: its multidisciplinary approach; its emphasis on ecclesial resources; and its recognition that ethical reasoning is a part of discipleship. I shall comment on each in turn.

a) A multi-disciplinary method

The GOE syllabus models a multi-disciplinary approach to Christian ethics, explicitly calling on its teachers to engage with history, psychology, and sociology as well as detailed exploration of bible and doctrine. Such polyphony is marshalled to serve the vision of 'an intelligent Christian' (1974, 4), and the part played by the Church's ministers in helping people to sort out both personal and social dilemmas. The authors even draw attention to one unnamed institution that had 'a social worker with psychological competence taking a full part in the life and teaching of the college throughout its year' and offer a rationale for engagement with the social sciences (1974, 107, 132-34). It is undoubtable that engagement beyond the normal bounds of ecclesial culture is necessary for Christian ethics today, as it was 50 years ago. And, indeed, it's hard to imagine that a single reader of this essay would disagree: each of us knows it is necessary to have a good grasp of the history and philosophy of our chosen field, whether medicine, politics, environmental science, psychology etc. and even better to bring in expert representatives of those fields, where possible, to share the teaching (I have benefitted greatly from co-teaching ethics at the end of life with a palliative care nurse for the past five years, for example). What I think is more inviting in this syllabus is the vision for a coherent moral theology that conjoins the often-detached facets of the theological task.

Otto Weber highlighted something similar when he described the twentieth century Western tradition of separating our treatment of the Christian life from the doctrinal substance of Christianity – an effort to 'make ethics autonomous' and to seek 'special criteria available for ethics' that are 'non-theological' (Weber, 1981, 63-8). It stemmed, he thought, from the Enlightenment's fragmentation of theology through increasing methodological specialization and particularization: biblical studies became dominated by historical criticism; pastoralia operated in the realms of sociology and psychology; and doctrine was caught up with philosophy. Such descriptions are limited by caricature, and all is not as it was, but that doesn't make the story Weber tells any less true. Specialist methodologies made cross-fertilization trickier, and theological sub-disciplines can become easily siloed.

What the 1974 GOE syllabus offers is only a direction of travel, but it aims beyond fragmentation. For example, its marshalling of the scholarship of (at that time) prominent New Testament scholars such as CH Dodd within the ethics classroom rather than in a biblical studies seminar is important. It indicates a more holistic dynamic, taking seriously the idea that 'all theological statements have ethical meaning' (Lehman, 1963, 238) as well as reminding students how to handle biblical material with appropriate insight and judgement. Teachers of ethics do well when we are theological polyglots, speaking the languages of biblical studies, doctrine, church history, pastoral studies, and (though not well represented in the syllabus) liturgical studies and sacramental theology as well. It will help our students develop an integrated understanding of the Christian life.

b) An ecclesial ethic
The GOE syllabus helpfully recognised that the church is a community within a community. It exists within a wider world of competing ideas. While there are undoubtedly places of overlap between the church and the wider world, the approaches to dealing with them are distinct. The ethical deliberation that the syllabus describes is primarily a shared enterprise of communal reason undertaken by those with shared faith in Jesus Christ. This is then extended and applied to the wider context by those same Christians as they live within it (see Leyden,

2019, 29-50). Such normativity is what makes Christian ethics *Christian*: 'the ethical teaching of the New Testament is dependent upon the theological teaching of the New Testament, on the church's theological interpretation of the events concerning Jesus, and its theological understanding of itself. The working out of these...was one of the major circumstantial influences on the formation of Christian ethics' (1974, 23). To put it another way, there are no separate criteria by which we might make sense of life other than those inherent to our faith (Weber, 1981, 68). It is not the same for people outside the Church, and we must be honest about that.

The GOE syllabus was on a trajectory of helping future priests be realistic about the post-Christendom context in which ethical issues must be considered. Secularists have long announced the break-down of Christian Europe and the evidence of declining influence of the Church in our common life is significant. Though decline was possibly accelerated by events of the twentieth century, intergenerational decline existed prior to them and has worsened since (Crockett and Voas, 2006). There is tension in the GOE syllabus as it wrestles with this. It aspires to form priests who would minister 'in church and out of church...in houses, schools, offices, factories or elsewhere; in pastoral guidance; and in their contribution to...social and political issues whether in their own locality or of public concern further afield' (ACCM, 1974, 89), but does not account for the growing reality that priests may not be invited to do so. In 1969 a Gallup Poll showed that two thirds of the British population thought the Church and her ministers should keep out of 'day to day social and political questions' (Field, 2015, Table 105). By 1990, the same number thought the church's view on social issues inadequate or irrelevant (2015, Table 77). Clergy were becoming much less a part of the fabric of society than they had been.

Perhaps that it why the syllabus articulates Christian ethics in the mode of crisis – responding to what Michael Banner calls 'the ethics of hard cases' (Banner, 2016, 8-13). This is shorthand for the specific issues worthy of ethical deliberation, and the sort the syllabus suggests were thrown up by technological advances, expanding industry, sexual liberation, and global change during the long sixties (1957-75). Attending to the hard cases might allow the church a distinctive contribution to the discussion, which is clearly important for the Established Church. But, at the same time it begs the question, what do Christians have to say about life when we are not dealing with the hard cases? How can ethical discourse help then? The syllabus is quieter at this point, which is telling. It puts me in mind of Banner's warning against ethics becoming 'so besotted with the hard cases as to take the view, in effect, that they comprise the scope of its tasks and responsibilities' (Banner, 2016, 9). Christian ethics is bigger than crises. It must also offer a thick description of the whole of life, an account of what the living well looks like when we are not navigating difficult issues as well as when we are, and thus a map of the terrain wherein our specific deliberations happen. It will marshal the doctrinal, biblical, historical, liturgical, and sacramental to outline the contours of a life orientated toward Jesus Christ and offer a vision of human flourishing to benefit both co-believers and interested persons outside the faith who are wondering what it's all about. We have seen the negative impact of the church becoming an 'issues based' contributor to public discourse in recent decades: without the bigger picture, our interjections can seem crass and at odds with the concerns of the society at large. For those of us teaching ethics today, we want to avoid introspection by seeking to equip ministers to explicate the Christian vision of human life to the church's friends and neighbours (ACCM, 1974, 91).

c) A discipleship tool
The GOE syllabus deliberately focused on teaching ordinands and trainee ministers. It offered tools for ethical deliberation that would operate principally in a community of non-specialists. Much academic theology is done for intellectual peers and colleagues, but the task of teaching ordinands is a responsibility to serve the whole church as it is instantiated in a parish. Hence the final section of the syllabus connected with pastoralia and sacramental ministry (1974, 112-15). While this section was very short, the trajectory is helpful: the goal of teaching ordinands is the formation of parishioners as disciples of Christ (see Leyden, 2019, 165-82). Alexander Schmemann argued that the tools of this formation are the materials of ministry: liturgy, Word, and sacrament. These three together create theologically textured space within everyday life, in which people are shaped and moulded through worship (Schmemann, 1973). If ethics is about how to live well and not just how to handle hard cases, then it too will need to make overt connection with these formational materials.

The implication of this, I think, is inviting. While parishioners may not read Augustine or Calvin or have time to wade through scholarly tomes on medical ethics or climate science, they do have significant experience of corporate liturgical prayer, recitation of the creeds, and celebration of the sacraments. These materials have significant moral value: they describe creaturely reality and God's vision for human flourishing in Christ. Drawing them into teaching and learning in our theological colleges inducts ordinands into the kind of work they will be required to do on the other side of ordination.

The Revd Dr Michael J Leyden is Dean of Emmanuel Theological College, in NW England, where he teaches at the interface of Christian doctrine and ethics, and Associate Minister of St Peter's Church, Chester.

Questions for discussion

1. "Christian ethics is bigger than crises." It is argued here that ethics is about the whole of life directed towards Jesus Christ in which the biblical, sacramental, doctrinal and liturgical dimensions of Christian life all play their part. How far has this larger landscape for Christian ethics been revealed during the crisis of Covid-19 and what has the crisis also revealed about the health of Christian ethical thinking more generally?

2. If Christian ethics is best regarded not as a subset or species of ethics more generally, but derives from "Christianity's peculiar worldview", how is ethical debate best encouraged or shaped in contemporary society so that Christians and others with a religious worldview may contribute?

References

Advisory Council for the Church's Ministry (ACCM), 1974, *Teaching Christian Ethics*, London: SCM.

Banner, M., 2016, *The Ethics of Everyday Life: Moral Theology, Social Anthropology, and the Imagination of the Human*, Oxford: Oxford University Press.

Brewitt-Taylor, S., 2018, *Christian Radicalism in the Church of England and the Invention of the British Sixties 1957-70: The Hope of a World Transformed*, Oxford: Oxford University Press.

Crockett, A., and Voas, D., 2006, 'Generation of Decline: Religious Change in Britain' in the *Journal for the Scientific Study of Religion* 45 (4) 567-84.

Field, C., *Religion in Great Britain 1939-99: A Compendium of Gallup Poll Data*, British Religion in Numbers Working Paper 2, http://www.brin.ac.uk/wp-content/uploads/2011/12/Religion-in-Great-Britain-1939-99-A-Compendium-of-Gallup-Poll-Data.pdf, Accessed Nov.2020.

Guroian, V., 1994, *Ethics After Christendom: Towards and Ecclesial Christian Ethic*, Grand Rapids: Williams B. Eerdmans.

Harries, R., Correspondence with the Author, 5th October 2020.

Lehman, P., 1963, *Ethics in a Christian Context*, Westport: Greenwood Press.

Leyden, M., 2019, *Faithful Living: Discipleship, Creed, and Ethics*, London: SCM Press.

Platten, S., 2013, 'Studying Christian Ethics: The Birth of the Society for the Study of Christian Ethics and the Context Out of Which It Grew' in *Studies in Christian Ethics* 26 (2) 205-223.

Reiss, R., 2013, *The Testing of Vocation: 100 Years of Ministry Selection in the Church of England*, London: Church House Publishing.

Schmemann, A., 1973, *For the Life of the World*, New York: St Vladimir's Press.

Weber, O., 1981, *The Foundations of Dogmatics: Volume 1*, Grand Rapids: Eerdmans.

Brave New World

Are We Amusing Ourselves to Death?

GRAHAM JAMES AND JAN MCFARLANE

A dystopian failure

In autumn 2020 Sky broadcast nine episodes of *Brave New World,* a series based on Aldous Huxley's novel, adapted significantly but with recognizable core themes and characters for those who know the original. First shown earlier in 2020 in the United States the series was commissioned by NBCUniversal for its streaming service Peacock. Peacock cancelled the commission after the first series. This was not going to run and run.

Anyone who watched it may not be too surprised. The characters lacked depth. The futuristic sets which combined sterility with brutalist architecture were scarcely pleasing. Even the orgies seemed to bore those involved. Yet these were the very things which struck me as indicating a significant degree of faithfulness to the book. Whenever a resident of New London in *Brave New World* experiences a disturbing emotion or even a slight degree of suffering, they take some Soma, a drug universally prescribed to ensure a sense of well-being. The people who live in this *Brave New World* are one dimensional. They cannot become interesting characters for the very reason that they are living without pain and suffering. That's one of the points of Huxley's book. It felt as if the commissioners and creator of the series had not reckoned with the nature of the material. The series killed itself. Huxley's *Brave New World* heralds the death of humanity as we know it. The really chilling thing is that these beings do not realize that what made them authentically human has died within them.

Perhaps it is almost impossible to portray *Brave New World* adequately on film or television because the medium itself is part of the problem. Turning *Brave New World* into televisual entertainment means the message of the novel is itself undermined and its ironies much less easy to identify. A further problem is that what seemed far-fetched when Huxley's novel was published in 1932 seem less bizarre now. The picture of life in New London in the recent Sky series was not totally unrecognizable. Huxley's novel is even more disturbing now than when it was written. We seem to be living it out.

Orwell or Huxley?

The sales of dystopian novels soared when President Trump was inaugurated in 2017, *Brave New World* among them. However, it was George Orwell's *1984* which saw the biggest increase. It has consistently outsold *Brave New World* ever since its publication in 1949 although it is the earlier novel which seems the more prescient. *Brave New World* was completed before the Nazis rose to power, the Second World War took place, the Cold War began, and the nuclear threat loomed large. By contrast in *1984* the political system is an overblown version of Stalinist totalitarian Communism, eager to control and suppress. This was a chilling reality in the late 1940s. If *1984* resembles anywhere in the contemporary world it is North Korea. When Orwell wrote his most famous novel rationing was worse than it had been in wartime so it may have seemed particularly unlikely that people would be controlled through entertainment, pleasure, distraction and superficiality. A police state with control over food supplies and propaganda seemed much more plausible. Even at the time, however, Huxley, in writing to Orwell (his pupil at Eton where both were educated) reckoned his vision was the more likely scenario since he believed people would be easier to control if they came to love their own servitude, especially if they thought of it as freedom.

As the years roll on, Huxley's vision seems to be unfolding before us, although few of us believe we are personally being lured into his *Brave New World*. It may be that those of us who think we have the capacity to avoid our enslavement are suffering the greatest illusion. But there have been prophets who have seen the way things are going, most notably Neil Postman.

Postman the prophet

Neil Postman was Professor of Communication Arts and Sciences at New York University, and died in 2003. In 1986 he published *Amusing Ourselves to Death* which argued that television was gradually transforming Western culture (and cultures elsewhere too) into a single arena where everything in the public square, whether politics, religion, education, business and commerce, had been turned into a form of entertainment. Writing just after the year 1984 had come and gone, Postman noted that many commentators had observed that Orwell's dire warnings had not come to pass. He believed that the signs of self-congratulation in American culture were unjustified since it was Huxley's thesis in *Brave New World* which was coming to fruition instead. In his introduction to *Amusing Ourselves to Death* Postman wrote:

> "Orwell warns that we will be overcome by an externally imposed oppression. But in Huxley's vision, no Big Brother is required to deprive people of their autonomy, maturity and history. As he saw it, people will come to love their oppression, to adore the technologies that undo their capacities to think." (Postman, 1986)

In 2020, according to the research organization Neilson, the average American adult spent over 12 hours a day engaging with the media. "Engaging with the media" includes the use of live television, radio and digital consumption, visiting apps on a smartphone or tablet, and using the internet and game consoles. Neilson employs representative panels to gauge such activity but reading books, magazines or newspapers is not included, presumably regarded as marginal activities.

With that in mind, let us return to Postman writing in the mid-1980s.

> "What Orwell feared were those who would ban books. What Huxley feared was that there would be no reason to ban a book, for there would be no one who wanted to read one. Orwell feared those who would deprive us of information. Huxley feared those who would give us so much that we would be reduced to passivity and egoism. Orwell feared that the truth would be concealed from us. Huxley feared the truth would be drowned in a sea of irrelevance. Orwell feared we would become a captive culture. Huxley feared we would become a trivial culture." (Postman, 1986)

When Postman wrote, a movie actor, Ronald Reagan, was the American President. In our own age the American President has been a reality TV star whose businesses are in the leisure, entertainment and gambling sectors. Postman would not be surprised, although he was writing before the term "reality television" was coined, a curious phrase in itself since "reality" is not what it portrays at all.

Religion as entertainment

One may have expected the Christian Church to have been a bulwark against this flight from seriousness. "In the beginning was the Word". Even though the Word became flesh, the Church has not neglected to add to the output of serious words in our world. Indeed, the writer of John's gospel has a vision of the world being unable to hold all the books that could be written about the Word, Jesus Christ. The mission of the Church has frequently worn the clothes of education. We may think of the schools established by monastic orders centuries ago or the way so many mission stations in the nineteenth century connected evangelism with education. Whether at kindergarten level or in higher education the commitment of the Church, both Catholic and Protestant, to education in the West and elsewhere has been evident. When Philip Larkin described a church as "a serious house on serious earth" (Larkin, 1988) he did not think he was saying anything controversial. Rather, his sympathy was aroused by a sacred building which stood in rebuke to the triviality of the age.

Postman's conviction a generation ago was that religion was becoming as captive to the relentless drive towards entertainment and triviality as any other. His illustrations were not limited entirely to the tele-evangelists of his day but included examples from Roman Catholicism and Judaism.

However, Postman also claimed that it was in the Bible that he "found intimations of the idea that forms of media favour particular kinds of content and therefore are capable of taking command of a culture". He pondered the prohibition on images of God in the Decalogue. He found it compelling that "the God of the Jews was to exist in the Word and through the Word, an unprecedented conception requiring the highest order of abstract thinking". Our own age has moved largely from being word-centred to image-centred, which is perhaps why words alone need to be brief if attention is held, something keenly understood by those who created Twitter.

The Word made flesh

Postman was not a theologian so one may not expect him to have a doctrine of the incarnation, but this "conception requiring the highest order of abstract thinking", the Word, became flesh. While Jesus is recorded as being able to debate with the doctors of the law in the Temple even at the age of twelve, his teaching and preaching, as we receive it in the gospels, is both within an identifiable rabbinic tradition but very direct and frequently pithy too. The images in his parables of the Kingdom (and their economy with words) seem attuned to our age of social media. Much of the Sermon on the Mount would work as a series of tweets, although the Beatitudes also demand abstract thinking. But why was the Word made flesh at such a time and in such a context when the "reach" of his mission was so circumscribed and local? This thought occurred to Tim Rice in 1970 as he wrote the lyrics for *Jesus Christ Superstar* where Judas sings:

> "Why did you choose such a backward time in such a strange land?
> If you'd come today you would have reached a whole nation
> Israel in 4BC had no mass communication."

Tim Rice was writing well before the internet and social media, and before Neil Postman too.

One of the writers of this article is currently ministering at Lichfield Cathedral which was the first cathedral to be used as a Covid vaccination centre. She tweeted a photograph of a bucket, half a dozen plastic chairs and a bottle of disinfectant against the backdrop of the steps to the pulpit with the caption "cleaning chairs for Jesus" followed by an emoticon of a cheeky wink. It gained attention and prompted us to wonder what people found so engaging in this tweet and why this image and caption led to more serious reflection. Perhaps its virtue was that it played into one of the news stories of the day, was neither wordy nor overtly evangelistic, but with more than a hint of the message of the Word made flesh for those with eyes to see. Following Jesus is about wrapping a towel around you and washing dusty feet. Being a bishop is also about remaining a deacon. "Cleaning chairs for Jesus" may mean wiping chairs as an act of Christian service, although equally it may mean preparing a safe space for the next person to sit since that person is made in the image and likeness of God. These were among the reactions triggered by what could be easily dismissed as a trivial, if entertaining, tweet.

Social media, Twitter especially, can seem like an echo chamber since the only people who follow bishops, for example, are those who either want to know what a bishop may say or (in a few cases) hope to ridicule or troll them. Yet retweeting does mean that some messages reach wider, even universal, audiences well beyond anyone's circle of "followers". Most of us would have been unaware of President Trump's daily tweets if mainstream media had not given them a megaphone. Any analysis of social media, though, may question if through this activity we are "amusing ourselves to death". It feels as if the greater danger is that we will angrily shout each other into oblivion.

Television and the trivial

Postman said "the single most important fact about television is that people *watch* it……and what they like to watch are moving pictures – millions of them, of short duration and dynamic variety. It is in the nature of the medium that it must suppress the content of ideas in order to accommodate the requirements of visual interest".

Postman believed that "thinking does not play well on television". Television is a performing art. This is one of the reasons why Postman considered television to be geared to show business, a medium of entertainment, and ultimately one which is liable to trivialise a culture.

Perhaps this explains why broadcast worship has always proved so demanding for production teams, clergy and audiences alike. While radio seemed to lend itself to worship more easily (the Daily Service remains the longest running programme on the BBC), there has been a considerable diminution of televised worship across all channels in the United Kingdom – until the Covid pandemic when it returned every Sunday to the BBC as a public service. The bulk of televised worship during the pandemic, however, has been home or church produced via Zoom, Facebook or YouTube, and audiences have been much larger than may have been anticipated. A recent study in the Church of England suggested at least 300,000 regular viewers had been attracted to online services who had never previously attended church in person.

When much of this online worship began, it would be fair to say that production values were not high but audiences were forgiving, and seekers were intrigued since the disappearance of broadcast worship on terrestrial channels rendered it largely invisible to those who did not attend. Online worship attracted the curious. Even those of us well used to churchgoing, however, found the liturgy and sermons in many online services very wordy. This may reflect our shortened attention spans (something on which Postman comments) but it may be that the possibilities of art, music and visual imagery had not been imaginatively utilised. One of us has said the office regularly online with others and used a painting or a sculpture as a visual aid for a brief reflection utilising the technology and working with it. Perhaps this is no more than a contemporary form of the stained-glass window, icon or highly decorated walls of medieval churches. Words have never had it all their own way in a religion where the Word was made flesh.

The lost art of concentration

An article in *The Guardian* by Harriet Griffey in late 2018 quoted some research published that year by Ofcom, the UK telecoms and broadcasting regulator. Ofcom reported that people checked their smartphones on average every 12 minutes, with nearly half checking their phone within five minutes of waking up. Those with smartphones face frequent interruptions to their days through the receipt of a new email, social media post, text message or, even occasionally, a telephone call. *The Guardian* article referred also to research undertaken at London's Institute of Psychiatry as long ago as 2005 by Dr Glenn Wilson which suggested persistent interruptions and distractions in our daily lives had a similar impact to a loss of sleep, resulting in up to a 10-point fall in IQ, more than the impact of smoking marijuana. That research was contested, but it may be that we are keen to dismiss it because it is so unwelcome.

Someone who has picked up the mantle of Neil Postman is Nicholas Carr whose book *The Shallows,* first published in 2010, explored the impact of the internet upon our behaviour. Carr, an American academic working on the relationship of technology to the human mind and contemporary society, was prompted to work in this area through noting what was happening in his own life, particularly his growing incapacity to read a book attentively.

> "Immersing myself in a book or a lengthy article used to be easy. My mind would get caught up in the narrative or the turns of the argument, and I'd spend hours strolling through long stretches of prose. That's rarely the case anymore. Now my concentration often starts to drift after two or three pages. I get fidgety, lose the thread, begin looking for something else to do. I feel as if I'm always dragging my wayward brain back to the text. The deep reading that used to come naturally has become a struggle." (Carr, 2010)

We recognize the phenomenon. While lockdown during the pandemic led us to expect to read a great deal more it has been surprisingly fitful. Even when distractions do not present themselves, we seem to search for them. Yet the desire to read books has not disappeared, so Huxley's prophecy has not quite come true. Nor does it seem to be fulfilled in wider society where book sales have been high. Whether books bought equates to books read is another matter, of course. The constantly changing, ephemeral nature of much of the increased communication of which we are part may be the cause for the diminution in our concentration. Postman contended that the means of transmission was not a matter of indifference. About that he was right, but it may not be that we are *amusing* ourselves to death. Perhaps the problem is that we have lost both the art of listening and a capacity for discernment. We have all become broadcasters and writers. Even the least literate social media user is mostly on transmit.

Universal deafness

In a sermon in Lichfield Cathedral in January 2021, the Canon Chancellor, Gregory Platten, reflected upon the concluding month of President Trump's term of office, and the storming of the Capitol. He observed that, from the beginning of his campaign to be President in 2015, Donald Trump had proclaimed that he would "build a wall". His final days in office were spent in a White House with a wall built around it. His main means of communication with the world via his Twitter account was closed down. Suddenly he was walled in both physically and metaphorically, silenced, disempowered.

President Trump was not unique in his use of social media. It is simply that he was the best known of all those who are on constant transmission. As Gregory Platten observed in that sermon a society where transmission is preferred over reception gradually becomes one incapable of listening. It becomes more divided because of deafness. We speak but do not listen. We write but do not read. Neither Huxley nor Postman would be likely to be surprised that this may be the way things are playing out.

How should Christians respond? Not by abandoning the culture and fleeing to hermitages and monasteries in the desert, though these have their place just as they did in the early Christian centuries. Nor by living in an Amish like exile in the society of our time. Discipleship sometimes demands a costly counter offensive to what divides us from those we live among. The meaning of *diabolos* is "to throw apart, separate, divide" which is what slanderers and accusers seek to do. Opposition to the Devil and all his works thus involves striving for unity. Christians are called to listen, discern, read, be mocked sometimes for being serious, but most of all to put on the towel of service and clean chairs as well as wash feet.

Neither Aldous Huxley nor Neil Postman had any solution to offer to the problems they diagnosed. Nor do the promises of Christ solve every problem for his disciples. But Christianity is a religion of the incarnation, one in which disciples are called to live within the world rather than reject it. But living in the world does not mean being conformed to it, as St Paul was keen to tell the Romans. "Do not be conformed to this world, but be transformed by the renewing of your minds, so that you may discern what is the will of God – what is good and acceptable and perfect." (Romans 12.2)

Perhaps the paraphrase by Eugene Peterson in *The Message* renders Paul's sentiment even more pertinently for our own age.

"Don't become so well-adjusted to your culture that you fit into it without even thinking. Instead, fix your attention on God. You'll be changed from the inside out. Readily recognize what he wants from you, and quickly respond to it. Unlike the culture around you, always dragging you down to its level of immaturity, God brings the best out of you, develops well-formed maturity in you." (Peterson, 2002)

> Graham James was Bishop of Norwich from 1999 to 2019.
> Jan McFarlane was Bishop of Repton from 2015 to 2020
> and is now Canon Custos of Lichfield Cathedral and an
> Honorary Assistant Bishop in the Diocese of Lichfield.

Questions for discussion

1. "Where is the wisdom we have lost in knowledge? Where is the knowledge we have lost in information?" So wrote T.S. Eliot in his *Choruses from the Rock* in 1934. Was he being prophetic in relation to modern communication or does what he said apply in any age?

2. How do you know if you are "so well-adjusted to your culture that you fit it without even thinking" and what resources do Christians have to avoid that trap?

References

Aldous Huxley, *Brave New World,* Chatto & Windus, 1932
George Orwell, *1984*, Secker & Warburg, 1949
Neil Postman, *Amusing Ourselves to Death*, William Heinemann, 1986, https://www.theguardian.com/lifeandstyle/2018/oct/14/the-lost-art-of-concentration-being-distracted-in-a-digital-world
Nicholas G. Carr, *The Shallows*, W.W. Norton & Co., 2010
Eugene Peterson, *The Message*, Navpress, 2002

Forum

Church and Kingdom

STEPHEN PLATTEN

What is the point of mission? There is undoubtedly a real divergence in the way this question is answered, which is perhaps most clearly seen in contrasts between certain expressions of 'evangelical theology' and theological reflection emerging from 'catholic' expressions of the Christian faith. It is often described by making a relatively sharp distinction between Church and Kingdom, which we shall encounter a little further on, and which concerns what the Church is and what it understands itself to be for.

This divergence was captured classically in an article in the journal 'Theology', back in 1979. The article was by Paul Gibson, a Canadian Anglican theologian and was titled *A Partisan Plea for Liberal Mission*. We shall not try to precis the piece here, but instead simply describe the aim of his article. His key point is that *liberal* and *liberality* imply an essential freedom to choose. Surely a liberal theologian would not want to press anyone or indeed proselytise anyone, since surely that stands in absolute contradiction to the very word liberal. The irony, at the same time, is that liberal Christians would hope that as many people as possible might also be attracted to the gospel of our Lord Jesus Christ, clothed in the same liberal garments as themselves. That may seem to be something of a caricature, but it is not far from the essence of the partisan plea for which Gibson argues.

The divergence implied here often focuses on whether the Christian faith requires each individual to give their life to Christ or whether it is about the cosmic transformation of our humanity. But the disagreement is not simply about individual versus corporate salvation, although that is part of the story. This bifurcation between the individual and the full mass of humanity is itself an oversimplistic and distorted view of the nature of the Christian message. In fact, the two things together are very clearly reflected as far back as in the theology of St Paul. So, for example, in Romans 7, Paul sharply defines that battle which goes on in each individual's soul:

> 'I do not understand my own actions. For I do not do what I want, but I do the very thing I hate......who would deliver me from this body of death? Thanks be to God through Jesus Christ our Lord.'

Here, Paul directly acknowledges the individual challenge and the promise of 'justification' or 'right-wising' as Rudolf Bultmann put it in rather ugly terms. Individuals are challenged to respond to Christ. But Paul also sees the crucial significance of the corporate, or universal aspect of what God has done for humanity in Christ. It is perhaps most richly stated in the much-quoted words from the fifth chapter of the Second Letter to the Corinthians:

> 'Therefore, if anyone is in Christ, they are a new creation; the old has passed away, behold the new has come. All this is from God, who through Christ reconciled us to himself and gave us the ministry of reconciliation; that is, God was in Christ reconciling the world to himself, and entrusting to us the ministry of reconciliation.'

A similar message emerges in the first chapter of the Letter to the Colossians, whether we believe it to have been written by Paul, or by a very close disciple. Here we are challenged by the entire 'Christ Event', or what Bultmann described as the 'salvation occurrence'. This was an event of cosmic, universal proportions; it was nothing less than a transformation of our humanity into the nature of Christ himself.

Thus far, in all that has been said, there has been no reference to Church or to Kingdom. Where do we find it in Holy Scripture? Of course, in the later New Testament writings, some notion of the Church, *ecclesia*, as a gathered community, does emerge, and certainly in the gospels, *Kingdom* is an essential concept, although it is not immediately translatable into a 'kingdom theology', as that term is so often used in Christian social ethics. Nonetheless, without doubt, the concept of *reconciliation* is central in both Testaments. This in itself implies an imperative issuing from the gospel.

This brings us to the work of a key theologian who speaks to this whole debate, Frederick Denison Maurice, an Anglican writing in the nineteenth century and one of the founders of a proto-Christian Socialism. Maurice was ever the controversialist. Son of a Unitarian minister, he became an Anglican and initially embraced the teaching of the 'Oxford Movement', later rebelled against Tractarianism to some extent. He taught in a number of institutions, eventually becoming Professor of English Literature and History and then Theology at King's College, London. Later he was stripped of his Chair – partly on account of his Christian Socialism but perhaps more importantly because of the impact of his writing in both *The Kingdom of Christ* and in his *Theological Essays*, which were both seen as falling short of orthodoxy. Almost certainly too, misunderstanding arose from his writing style, which is extraordinarily convoluted and notable for its prolixity.

In terms of our focus here, perhaps most crucial of all was his writing on ecclesiology, that is, his understanding of the Church and sacraments. His teaching on baptism takes us to the heart. In a letter to a Quaker friend, he broaches the subject head on, rejecting what he sees as the claims of Evangelicals. He then similarly offers a critique of Pusey and the Tractarians, whom he misrepresents to a degree or perhaps simply misunderstands. Evangelical teaching is rejected because of its rootedness in the faith of the individual. What he believed to be the Anglo-Catholic approach is rejected because of its apparent insistence on baptism bringing about a change in the nature of our humanity.

But what did Maurice himself believe? In this letter to his Quaker friend, he writes:

> 'In my last letter I maintained that Christ, by whom, and for whom, all things were created, and in whom all things consist, has made reconciliation for mankind.[1]

So, for Maurice, already established in Christ's work, is a relationship between every human being and God in Christ, right from that person's birth onwards. In other words, we are born into a state of grace. Baptism pours further grace into that relationship as the person becomes part of the community of the Church. Such teaching dismisses the terror of infant children dying outside a state of grace having died before being baptised. Jeremy Morris summarises F D Maurice's view thus:

> 'Baptism begins the believer's life in the *Kingdom* and instantiates for the believer a union with God already true through the reconciling life and ministry of Jesus Christ. Baptism, for Maurice was egalitarian,

in that it dispensed with the idea of all spiritual gradations between human beings. All human beings had a spiritual 'eye' which could be closed by self-will, or opened through baptismal fellowship.'[2]

Thus, every individual effectively is welcomed into the Kingdom at birth but not sacramentally incorporated into the Church. Church and Kingdom are not the same – Kingdom is a broader concept and does not bring with it the sacramental elements of faith which are essential to any ecclesiology.

Elsewhere Jeremy Morris writes:

'It was a fundamental axiom of Maurice that God had created human beings for communion with each other and with himself. This relationship constituted the primary truth of theology under which all other doctrines stood.'[3]

Having then set out Maurice's approach, this offers a foundation for our understanding of the sharp division of opinion on personal and corporate salvation, which we encountered earlier. Maurice argues that God's love is there for us from our birth, God is already working for the Kingdom, going before us; *we* do not establish the Kingdom for God. We are offered the choice of working with God for the Kingdom into which we are joined in baptism.

How might this affect our view of the Church? Let us bring on the next witness in the person of the German Protestant theologian, Ernst Troelstch, who was writing in the early years of the twentieth century. Troeltsch's work straddled the boundaries between theology and sociology. Here we shall focus only on his understanding of sociological models of the Church and the implications of these for ecclesiology. Troeltsch saw two main divergent models which he believed described different understandings of the Church – he calls these the *communal* and *associational* models. The communal pattern assumes, after the mould of F D Maurice, that all human beings are from the beginning created in and for God's grace – we are all born into a relationship with God in Christ. Thus, the communal model assumes both that God is already in the world working to establish the kingdom, and that therefore every human being is the responsibility of, and lies within the focus of, the Church's apostleship and ministry. Of course, individuals may deliberately exclude themselves from the Church's purview either by 'closing their spiritual eyes by their own self-will' (to use Maurice's phrase) to the path of faith, or by being adherents of a different creed or faith community. This inclusive approach has been very much the pattern followed by the Church of England since the Reformation.

The *associational* view of the Church is rooted in differing models of a gathered community, of an eclectic church. Here, in its most extreme form, the church sees its role as the agency that snatches individuals as brands from the burning fires of hell or brings them safely into the ark of the faithful and thus into a 'personal relationship with Jesus'. As the impact of secularisation has increased, so has the attractiveness of this second model correspondingly increased. The implied 'liberalism' of the communal model is seen to be too complacent, insufficiently proactive in terms of the salvation of individual souls. Effectively it was this associational model that governed the drafters of the Church of England report *Mission-Shaped Church*. Undoubtedly, when well organised, churches founded on this model can be highly 'successful', albeit exclusive in approach and unashamedly understanding themselves as a gathered church. Baptism is the one and only gateway to salvation.

Each of these models will perforce beget a different pattern of mission. The associational *modus operandi* will focus primarily on increasing the numbers in the pews – that is the aim and effectively the starting point: mission means more people. Other implications will follow but this is the primary focus, alongside the nourishing of the internal life of the community. Such an approach most often uses the phrase *being church* – it is crucial to note the omission of the definite article there. Through that omission, 'church' becomes an end in itself. It produces an inner-directed pattern where all the rigmarole of church (too often seen as a club for those of a like mind) consumes the life of the community. The aim was outreach but effectively the result is 'in-reach'. In a moment we shall see the impact of retaining the definite article and speaking of 'the church', or better still 'the *Church*', by which one is identifying with the Church universal and not one self-contained local community.

The *communal* model sees mission through the lens of care and engagement with the whole community ,working for the Kingdom – being *the Church* – now applies – such a phrase requires a predicate; what are we being the Church for…? To leave the phrase 'the Church' hanging with no predicate is vacuous – the Church is called to be the instrument of God in Christ in the world, working with God to build the Kingdom. That is what the Church is for. Through care and witness to Christian values - sometimes requiring political action - and often challenging assumptions in the ambient culture – then, the Church, it is argued, will draw others to Christ. The curtains opened in the last generation, in terms of the `Church of England, with an initiative set precisely within this perspective in the form of the report commissioned by the then Archbishop of Canterbury, *Faith in the City*. It is a classic derivative of the communal approach which led to the establishment of the *Church Urban Fund* and provoked government to take action in the inner cities.

On my arrival in West and South Yorkshire, as Bishop of Wakefield, similar challenges beckoned. Grimethorpe, the place where the film *Brassed Off* was set, is one of the most powerful examples of the challenges which the local church, that is the diocese, had to face at that time. Grimethorpe had been a thriving community of some 13,000 souls. By the time of my arrival, twenty years after the divisive Miners' Strike, with deep mining now almost gone, Grimethorpe was down to just 7,000 inhabitants, with a decimated community spirit. Those who *had work* drove off daily to warehouses on the M62 – but many were *workless* and not *unemployed* – by now there were some families who had been living through two generations with worklessness. The impact on the social psychology of that pit village was devastating. Here then was the first focus for the Church and its ministry and mission.

Its only immediate resources were the parish priest and a rather barn-like Victorian church building. Father Peter Needham was a charismatic character (using that word in its non churchy sense) and he immersed himself in the community. Early on I was invited to preach at Evensong and then carry the Blessed Sacrament through the entire village, finishing at the Working Mens' Club, the old miners' gathering place, where I gave benediction to a packed house. All along our route, people had crowded in the streets to be part of this spectacle, but more than that, this was a symbol of renewal. Alongside this we worked with local doctors, social services and community groups – most of them led by women. (Arthur Scargill's estranged wife was a GP and churchgoer – Scargill himself was by now 'persona non grata' in much of the former mining community of this part of South Yorkshire). We were able to assist in the process of drawing down grants for renewal and social support. Eventually the interior of the church building was adapted for other uses without interfering with the main worship space. Here was a communal church pattern exemplified. Here there was a clear sense of working for the Kingdom; the local church saw its role as seeking out God's presence and working with the God of our Lord Jesus Christ in the community. Interestingly enough, gradually the congregation grew – not exponentially but significantly – in what had before seemed a very Godless climate.

Alongside what I have described thus far, we all also owe much in this area to Roman Catholic social teaching, reaching back for more than a century to Pope Leo XIII's ground-breaking encyclical, *Rerum Novarum*. Teaching issuing from the concept of the *Common Good* has been seminal and is rooted in a communal view of mission. Two other notable writers outside the Roman Catholic Church showing a similar communal focus include Reinhold Niebuhr in the USA with his emphasis on *Christian Realism*, and with his challenging, seminal 1932 book, *Moral Man and Immoral Society*, which indicated a radical difference in the behaviour of groups as opposed to individuals in relation to politics and social ethics. From the Anglican stable, perhaps the key contributor was William Temple who was a member of the Beveridge Committee whose work presaged the emergence of the 'Welfare State' and the 1944 Education Act. Temple's *Christianity and the Social Order* sowed the seeds for this development, and Temple and Niebuhr were reciprocally interdependent! Temple's concept of 'middle axioms' attempted to apply a 'Kingdom theology' which allowed Christian values to be applied to the life of society as a whole – a thoroughly communal model.

Of late, another challenging model has emerged with the work of the American theologian Stanley Hauerwas. Hauerwas is trenchantly critical of 'liberal' models including those of Niebuhr and Temple. He argues that engaging with the values of contemporary culture compromises the challenge of Christian theology and indeed Christology (ironically there is overlap with the very different starting point of John Milbank and the 'radical orthodox' school). Instead, Hauerwas argues, the Church must simply 'be the Church' and, if its life and witness has a challenging impact on society, then so be it, but the essence of the gospel can be the only starting point. Such an approach has different implications. Nonetheless, these two models need not be entirely confrontational or mutually exclusive, as has been demonstrated recently.[4]

As a Church of England deacon, priest and bishop, I admit to remaining entirely committed to the communal model of the Church and the patterns of mission that it implies. All people fall within the gracious love of God in Christ, all are part of the responsibility of God's Church – not, of course just the Church of England! Nonetheless, there is no doubt that an ideological application of this principle will have its own serious flaws. A concern for a growing Church with a healthy and growing kernel is essential if the gospel is to survive. We can learn from elements within the associational model and should not simply discount all concern with the salvation of individuals and their relationship with their Creator and Redeemer.

New ways of attracting more to the Church community are essential, for example through pilgrimage and other initiatives including street theatre, political engagement, dramatic portrayal of *The Way of the Cross*, and much more. There is no philosophy more illiberal than that of the fundamentalist liberal! We must remain open to learn from those with whom we most vehemently disagree.

Stephen Platten, Berwick-upon-Tweed.

An earlier version of this article was presented to the Annual Meeting of the Urban Theological Union in Sheffield, in November 2020.

Notes
1. *To Build Christ's Kingdom: F.D.Maurice and his Writings.* Edited by Jeremy Morris. Canterbury Press, London.2007.p.95
2. Jeremy Morris, *F D Maurice and the Crisis of Christian Authority.* Oxford University Press, Oxford.2005.p.82.
3. Op cit.p.64
4. Cf. for example Matthew Bullimore 'Public Theology or Ecclesial Theology', in *Theology Reforming Society: Revisiting Anglican Social Theology.* SCM Press, London.2017. pp.144-166.

Reviews

Christianity and the New Spirit of Capitalism
Kathryn Tanner
Yale University Press, 2019, x + 241 pp., hbk, £20.99

Kathryn Tanner has always been a theologian who is hard to pin down and pigeonhole. She has allies and friends but no team or club. She does, however, have themes. Like Springsteen returning to an acoustic record between street band albums, Tanner returns to advance and explore her theological agenda *vis à vis* the economic dimensions of human life. In 2005 she first laid this out in the *Economy of Grace*, which translated her doctrinal focus into a theological economy focusing on non-competitive possession and universal giving in stark contrast to capitalism. She has returned now for a further, more forensic exploration; offering a more detailed 'how it works' sort of analysis of our precise capitalist moment and a contrast with basic Christian commitments.

Tanner advances her theological account of economic life with precision. She presents not a general capitalism but rather dissects very carefully what she calls 'finance driven capitalism' (FDC) and its particular implications. This makes her case for its antithetical relation to Christianity much more compelling. She establishes this first by clearly distinguishing FDC from Industrial Capitalism (IC) and Weber's analysis of the Protestant work ethic. For all its destructive consequences, IC was a much friendlier form of capitalism, protecting workers in some, albeit limited and hard-won, ways and restricting greed and consumption. Its mutated sibling, FDC, has no such protections or restrictions. One of the key differences is that whilst workers under IC could credibly expect a future reward or return for their labours, workers under FDC live in the perpetual insecurity of constantly deferred reward – a continuous and never completed cycle of work. This is a change of worldview or way of life as much as of industrial practices. The lack of security and the demands of productivity mean work demands the full attention and total commitment of the worker. The mobility of capital means responsibility for production and survival rests squarely on the shoulders of the workers; all are entrepreneurs or functionally self-employed, taking on the attendant risks. This fundamentally reorientates the lives of many millions of people in a way that reinscribes the value of human life itself. Dignity is derived from work, rather than the other way around.

The middle three chapters unpack this reorientation in detail through the lens of time. Past, present, and future collapse in this picture into a laborious and productivity-focused eternal present predicated on debts and responsibilities incurred in the past and never to be resolved in a perpetually deferred future. This analysis of time sets the stage for the central doctrinal commitments of Tanner's argument. Eschatology, Tanner argues, offers a fundamentally different relation of future to present. The promise of eschatology challenges the perpetual present chained to the past. Furthermore, this is a realised rather than deferred eschatology. The present is not the same as the future but the future is realisable in the present. Christians are called to live another present which embodies and prefigures the future. The three aspects of time are thus reformatted. The present, for Christians, cannot be dominated by the past on the basis of God's forgiveness. Nor can the present give its total commitment to productivity in the face of the call of discipleship to live only in total commitment to God. Lastly, the present is funded by a hope that comes from and goes towards a transformative future.

The cumulative effect of the basic Christian claims outlined above is what Tanner calls an 'anti-work ethic', which is the appropriate response to FDC (in contrast to the Weber's Protestant work ethic with IC.) In line with recent calls for a renewal of Sabbath, this separates human value from productivity and roots it more fundamentally in the *imago dei*. Who we are, rather than what we do, is of fundamental significance. And so the question is, who has FDC made us into and what does Christ call us to be?

Tanner offers little practical outworking of what resistance in line with these Christian commitments might look like. Her main task is diagnostic. She is rarely prescriptive in her proposals not least because, as she argues in *Theories of Culture*, Christian responses must always be concrete, particular, and contextual. Furthermore, she is hesitant of undermining the eschatological divine agency of the response by outlining a potentially Pelagian program for change. Resistance is something that should follow from discipleship well practiced. And

Reviews

here lies a potential weakness. It would seem obvious that this must be a corporate endeavour but the primary focus in this text seems more concerned with how individual Christians relate to salvation in contrast to work. Spelling out the form of Christians' corporate vocation further would have helped assuage some disappointments at the lack of practical proposals.

Ultimately, this is an excellent, forensic, diagnosis of a dominant force in the world globally. There is little room left for generalisations about capitalism. Tanner has spelled out its current guise and where, specifically, it challenges a Christian orientation within the world. The book is an excellent example of how doctrine, and discipleship, implies or directs practice, even if it doesn't offer a programme to follow as such.

Andrew Hayes
Queen's Foundation, Birmingham

Only God Will Save Us
Simon Cuff
SCM Press, 2020, xi + 240 pp., pbk, £19.99

In *Only God Will Save Us*, Simon Cuff gives us a book that is 'unashamedly theological', but also incredibly readable, accessible and actually quite exciting. After all, drawing on the riches of Christian orthodoxy, this is a book about who God is, what God does, and what that means for the world and the lives we lead. Without doubt, this is an entry level book on the doctrine of God, but that is not a weakness. Instead, this could be viewed as an easy to pick up, pocket guide to the nature of God and the Christian life. It's a page turner that leaves you wanting more, unpacking divine truths and providing 'aha!' moments of epiphany. But it also makes you think on after putting it down, and inspires you to action. Properly and well read, this book will lead the reader into the path of God and the transformative Christian life.

The first chapter on Divine Simplicity, provides a gentle but rigorous grounding for the rest of the book. It's a superbly crafted beginners guide to one of the key principles underlying the orthodox, classical doctrine of God. Cuff takes the reader through the key arguments and historical developments in a way that is clear, methodical and gentle. And that this is so should not be overlooked: Divine Simplicity, ironically, is not simple stuff. Yet Cuff does not allow the reader to be overwhelmed or undersold.

With the foundations firmly laid, Cuff then takes the reader through some of the challenges that have faced the classical doctrine of God over the centuries. He does this with real style, but also empathy. Never deriding a detractor, he gives their arguments a hearing, and respects the process through which their arguments were formed. But ultimately, he sensitively demonstrates the errors in their position. Cuff engages particularly well with Moltmann and Bonhoeffer here. He is generous and fair, but firm and confident in his rebuttals. One of the greatest strengths of this chapter (as well as the whole book), is the pastoral insight and the practical action encouraged, in light of the truth proclaimed. Cuff empathetically notes, for example, that God *understanding* our suffering isn't actually very helpful. Instead, God transforms suffering, and asks us to do likewise.

The call to do likewise is the practical outworking of the divine nature, according to Cuff, and that is illustrated with energy and fervour throughout the book, but perhaps most beautifully in the chapter on the love of God. Building on the doctrine of divine simplicity, Cuff emphasises God and God's love being one and the same, and unpacks this through the doctrine of the incarnation and what this means for humankind. For Cuff, the doctrine of God compels Christian action to be neither static nor self-interested, but intentional and involving the outpouring of our whole selves.

The chapter on prayer feels like something of a climax to the book. It is where it all begins and ends, where everything is tied together. It also offers the most practical and reassuring advice for the Christian life. Here Cuff draws from some of the best theologians throughout the ages, but with them is not afraid to ask (and address) some of the harder questions. One such question being 'why bother praying to an omnipotent and omniscient God at all?' For Cuff's answer you must read the book. But typically, Cuff puts the reader at ease. You don't feel patronised or pandered to, but nor do you feel daft or a failure. Cuff is honest and realistic about prayer, but he also inspires excitement about it. Here, the reader will receive sound advice about what good prayer might look like, clearing a path for personal and spiritual growth.

One of the oldest charges levelled at the classical doctrine of God is that it is really just the 'god of the philosophers', but Cuff avoids any such impression in this book. *Only God Will Save Us* is absolutely rooted in scripture and grounded in the early Church and its texts. It is also strengthened by engagement with some of the best theologians of modern times. As a result, this is not a book of heavy or stale theology. It is a book with the potential to transform and renew the faith of even the most mature Christians, while inspiring the most fledgling and enquiring. It is a breath of fresh air from a theologian whose writing is not partisan or derisory of other positions, but who has reached back into the riches of the Christian tradition and found gold. His earnest belief and passion are tangible in these pages, and they're infectious. More works like *this* on the beauty and truth of orthodox Christian doctrine are very welcome.

Tom Mumford
Diocese of St. Edmundsbury and Ipswich

Sabbath Rest: The Beauty of God's Rhythm for a Digital Age
Mark Scarlata
SCM Press, 2019, xi + 128 pp., pbk, £12.99

In *Sabbath Rest: The Beauty of God's Rhythm for a Digital Age*, Scarlata offers a series a 'reflections' on the gift of the Sabbath from someone who is 'not an expert but a fellow pilgrim', one who has been 'convicted of [his] own Sabbath neglect' (*x*). Scarlata's emphasis throughout is the *practice* of the Sabbath, encouraging his readers to reflect for themselves on how learning to inhabit a 'Sabbath-rhythm' (of six days of work and one day of rest) is central to creation's journey towards wholeness. As he reminds us, the Sabbath is 'as much about political and economic freedom as it is about physical and spiritual rest' (3). To this end, each chapter ends with four questions to aid the reader in reflecting on the Sabbath's significance, and the book is peppered with practical suggestions for maintaining the Sabbath. Nonetheless, Scarlata's purpose in this book is not to offer a guide for how to practise the Sabbath, but rather to 'explore the biblical texts to offer a compelling case for why the Sabbath remains critical to the life and witness of God's people today' (*x*).

Given Scarlata's expertise in biblical studies, it is unsurprising that he begins with an overview of how the Sabbath features in scripture, and how this both reflects and is reflected upon in Jewish and Christian practices of Sabbath observance. In the second half of Chapter 1, Scarlata pivots away from the scriptural account in order to look at the Sabbath 'through the lens of beauty' (25). By analogy with music, he suggests that the Sabbath provides us with a 'rhythm for life' through which we 'begin to discover the depths and riches of God's truth and beauty in the world' (25). Such rhythm both 'stabilizes and destabilizes' (30), enabling us to 'see God's glory and beauty in the repetitive and mundane as we catch glimpses of eternity' (33). This Sabbath-rhythm of work and rest, Scarlata suggests in Chapter 2, is built into God's act of creation. He suggests that this pattern 'reflects our participation with God [in both God's activity and rest] as those made in his likeness' (46). Specifically, Scarlata sees the Sabbath as a hallowing of time, through which we may 'attune our lives to the music of creation' (49). Such attunement provides a 'lens' through which we can 'begin to see life through the eternality of God's kingdom' (58).

Chapter 3, 'The Beauty of Liberation', is perhaps of greatest interest to readers of *Crucible*, for it reflects on how the Sabbath offers 'an alternative vision to the world of how to live as a community in relationship to others and in relationship to God' (66). The chapter opens with an account of the Sabbath as an alternative to social, political, and economic systems that exploit the poor and vulnerable, generate inequality, and drive us toward restless consumption. As Scarlata insists, the Sabbath is a 'gift for the liberated to bring liberation', in which our rest is about 'bringing justice to those around us' (67). The second half of the chapter extends these principles to our relationship with the land: 'to enter into the holiness of Sabbath time we are required to enter it together with the land' (80).

In the fourth chapter, Scarlata discusses how the Sabbath initiates us into a rhythm of trust in God's grace. He argues that the 'digital world does not allow for rest' because we are 'constantly switched on' (90). He suggests that stepping away from our digital lives for a day 'is no easy task for many' (92), whether that is because we fear that 'everything will completely fall apart if we are not always present or available' (92), because we fear that others 'might forget about us' (93), or because we have become 'so accustomed to constant noise and distractions that when they cease we are terrified of the silence and facing our own selves' (93).

The book culminates in an account of the Sabbath as a 'communal gift' (101), recognising that it is 'not difficult to turn the Sabbath day into a day of self-satisfaction and self-absorption' (105). He explores Isaiah's vision of the Sabbath community incorporating all people, and considers how this is picked up in the New Testament witness to Christ as a 'further unveiling of the rest that God had intended for all

Reviews

creation from the beginning of time' (116). This unfolds in a vision of the Sabbath as a sign of hope for the restoration and transformation of creation; '[i]n Christ', Scarlata suggests, 'Sabbath-keeping is a continued discipline of the Church to celebrate true rest and liberation coming into the world' (121).

Whatever the merits of this book, it is somewhat surprising, given its subtitle, that the book dedicates only four pages explicitly to the question of Sabbath observance in a digital age (90-94). A greater emphasis on this would have differentiated this work from existing Christian retrievals of the significance of the Sabbath (most notably, perhaps, Norman Wirzba's *Living the Sabbath*, and Walter Brueggemann's *Sabbath as Resistance*). Nonetheless, this work offers a helpful introduction to, and wise reflection upon, the implications of the Sabbath for lived practice.

Peter Leith
University of Cambridge

Imagining Mission with John V. Taylor

Jonny Baker & Cathy Ross
SCM Press, 2020, xiv + 160 pp., pbk, £19.99

As I approached this book, I was very conscious that I am not an Anglican, and that I know nothing about John V. Taylor. But I was intrigued by the title, and by one word in particular: *'imagining'*. Until recently I served as a District Mission and Evangelism Facilitator in the Methodist Church and in that role I found myself frequently asking questions such as: "How do we help churches have an imagination to do things differently?", "If the only model of mission that you know is the one you currently have, where does the imagination come from to try something different?" In response to those questions, this is the book I wish I could have put into the hands of every church I worked with – a relatively short read that manages to be both accessible and challenging.

Imagining Mission is drawn from Taylor's unpublished travel diaries, which informed his Newsletters written while General Secretary of the Church Missionary Society between 1963 – '74. The book is divided into three Parts, each reflecting a key theme from these writings: Church, Mission, and Society. It begins with an 'Intro', which sets the scene as Taylor 'encourages us to develop a posture of imagination, innovation and improvisation in mission' (xi), and ends with an 'Outro', which homes in on the theme of imagination as 'the currency of mission' (149). Each Part contains two chapters, with Baker writing on 'Church', Ross on 'Mission', and with each writing a chapter on 'Society', focusing on specific missional themes – the environment (Baker) and other faiths (Ross).

I did feel that the book suffers from something of an identity crisis: is it a book about developing the imagination and thinking creatively? Is it a book about mission? Or is it a book about John V. Taylor? And could a book of this length do justice to all three aspects of its title? It soon becomes clear that the main focus throughout is on the 'Imagining', with an 'Exercising Creativity' section at the end of each chapter designed to help spark and cultivate readers' imagination – the 'Outro' finally revealing this as the authors' intention. My disappointment was that as a result I did not really learn as much as I expected to about John V. Taylor, but as an introduction to his writings it serves well for those who are unfamiliar with them. However, the book would benefit from a short biography of Taylor, and a bibliography of his work to provide some context.

The heart and soul of the book is Part 2, 'Mission', with chapters three and four really quite breath-taking. In particular, Chapter 3 shows how ahead of his time Taylor was in his views on mission. For any student of mission, there is not much new here and yet I was surprised by how fresh this chapter seemed, and how relevant for our times – leaving the reader to wonder how different both the church and its mission might have been if more notice of his writings had been taken sooner. The title, 'An Adventure of the Imagination', taken from a reference in Taylor's *The Primal Vision*, really would be an apt sub-title for the book, describing well what the reader is invited into.

While each Part stands alone, a reordering of the book might have made for a better read. Beginning the book with 'Mission' would give a good foundation for the rest of the book as this Part sets the scene of Taylor's thinking on mission. 'Society' follows 'Mission' well, as these chapters ground Taylor's generalised thinking in the specific examples of the missional challenges posed by the environment and other faiths. As it was, Chapter 1 was a somewhat abrupt start to the book, and both chapters in this first part, on Church, seemed be less dependent on Taylor's thought. Had 'Church' come at the end after 'Mission' and 'Society', this would not only have helped the flow of argument, but 'Mission' coming before 'Church' also makes a theological statement. As

Reviews

Moltmann puts it: 'It is not the church that has a mission of salvation to fulfil to the world; it is the mission of the Son and the Spirit through the Father that includes the church, creating a church as it goes on its way' (*The Church in the Power of the Spirit*, 1977, p.64). I wonder what imaginings of Church might follow on from imaginings of mission?

This said, I am left inspired to read Taylor's work, and I hope that this book will inspire those who long to join in the adventure both of the imagination and of mission, but are unsure where to begin.

Rachel Deigh
Wesley House, Cambridge

Pilgrims and Priests: Christian Mission in a Post-Christian Society
Stefan Paas
SCM Press, 2019, xx + 257pp., pbk, £25

The post-Christian reality

There was a time when 'parish mission' meant a concentrated week in the calendar to reach out to the uncommitted or non-churchgoers, invite them to hear a guest speaker and befriend them with special events. Then by the late 20th century, that idea was replaced by mission as a permanent state of being – mission-shaped church, mission action plans, fresh expressions, church growth, messy church, cafe church, and now (lo and behold in the age of covid) *online church*.

Each initiative is hailed in its time as a new way to reach people, or a new method of evangelism. Growth and renewal have indeed happened in places over the last twenty years. The Church as a whole would have been poorer and smaller without some of these initiatives which have helped to slow or even reverse some church decline. Underlying them all, the ultimate aim of making new disciples, growing the Church, and even transforming a secular society, has remained more or less unchanged since the days when mission was an event rather than a process.

But secularisation, with the loss of Christian faith and influence across 'the West', has continued. The aims of mission, as carried over from the days of an unchallenged Christianity expanding its domain, have largely failed. Mission conceived in this way – winning the secular majority over to Christian allegiance – is no longer viable. Churches in the West, whatever their missionary strategies within their own cultures, must learn like the Apostle Paul (1 Corinthians 2) what it means to be 'foolish' and 'weak' in the world.

This is the starting point and fertile ground for Stefan Paas, professor of missiology and intercultural theology at Vrije Universiteit, Amsterdam, with other attachments in the Netherlands and in South Africa. He is unmistakably ecumenical, European and internationalist. Instead of hanging on to further dreams of reclaiming territory for Christianity, or indeed co-opting any residual folk religion, he sees *missional spirituality* as a key quality for the small minority communities in the West which the Church has become.

This book is not another litany of decline, nor is it one of the cheery textbook manuals telling us how to do mission in the modern age. Paas is not even trying to tell us how to re-imagine mission – which can be code for "now try this again". He is warmly instructive, but not concerned with how to grow the size of the Church or arrest its decline in 'the West'. We might want more precision about where and what counts as 'the West' or Western culture. The sociologists of religion can do that for us. But Paas is much more a theologian. With faith and insight, he faces the reality of Christianity as one world religion among many, and as a minority community in many non-religious countries. From this reality, he explores exile and diaspora, and the New Testament example of 1 Peter among others, as biblical categories for an outward-looking spirituality which does not revert to the failed ideologies of conversion and expansion.

Churches of pilgrim and priestly character

The title *Pilgrims and Priests* points to an understanding of the Church, as much as to a mode of mission. Paas barely mentions Avery Dulles, but those familiar with the Dulles analysis will recognise the influence of that approach to ecclesiology. For some, the pilgrim 'model' has become a bandwaggon for a loose mix of liberal and radical ideas. But it has also become identified with the counter-cultural self-realisation of a *movement* (a non-churchy church) which enjoys unclear boundaries and eclectic spirituality. Being pilgrims, for Stefan Paas, is counterbalanced by being priests. In the last two chapters on priestly witness and character, we find a strong echo of the old sacramental 'model'. But now it is offering not 'traditional church' but *signs and foretastes of the Kingdom,* because the Church now journeys on with a minority and unfulfilled status of pilgrims.

To be a priestly church, for Paas, has rather little to do with a ministerial priesthood. It is about the minority Christian community living their priestly, vicarious role, principally of prayer and praise, *on behalf of* the majority who cannot or do not want to be with them. Such a concept has in practice sustained many Western churches for generations, even back to the time when they were supposedly serving 'majority Christian' societies.

For those wanting to be refreshed by surveying the progress of missiology over the last fifty years, there are plenty of markers. The landmark *Transforming Mission* by David Bosch has notably reached its 24th edition (2008), while many other writers like Alasdair MacIntyre and Leslie Newbiggin are included in the wide range of important thought reflected by Paas. He tends to favour those who perceive a decisive divide between church and world, and has a fondness for the revival of radical Anabaptist thought, as in the writings of J.H.Yoder and Stanley Hauerwas. In the UK it is harder to discern where such fearless countercultural trends can be found.

For the churches, the question remains: how long will it take to adapt to the *implications for mission* of a Christianity which is sidelined in western society, and globally is now only one world faith among many? Can we acknowledge and live with the reality of being a minority community? How do we relate to a secular society which has become yet more indifferent, even hostile, to many forms of Christianity?

Missionary spirituality

Paas has plenty of confidence in Christian witness. But pilgrims and priests are not immune from questioning. Despite the widespread attractiveness of the pilgrim metaphor, pilgrims are not *just* 'on a journey' towards a better place. They have to mix with all sorts on the way. Counter-cultural need not mean anti-cultural. Not 'of the world', we might say, but still 'in it'. In it, surely, up to our necks. Pilgrims get their hands dirty as well as their feet.

Priests indeed had their place in the Jewish religion, but there were many other roles. Prophets have a far bigger biblical significance. A drawback with Paas's vision is that the prophetic and servant callings of a Christian community are too much taken for granted. Yes, priestly people can be servants and prophets too. But this moral vision, (especially for Crucible readers), needs to be addressed more fully, to nurture a missionary spirituality that will infuse minority Christian communities.

Still, inspired by the biblical experience of *exile,* and after spending more than a full chapter on the significance of exile and diaspora, Paas 'returns home' to a catholic version of the Church, albeit with primitive echoes. This Church is the way in which all Christians are nurtured by the worship and Eucharist at the heart of their life. Individualism is not welcome in this model of The Body of Christ, though Paas mercifully does not like the word 'model'. He is more straightforward in recommending the life of a minority community in a counter-cultural setting.

Is it enough?
While the original was in Dutch, he has rewritten this English edition with changes for an international audience. The style is easy and nicely pitched. Most chapters have the lively character of a spoken address. The footnotes and bibliography are extensive, meeting the needs of all types of students in this field. The structured sections of each chapter are well suited both to the general reader and to the task of reflective practice.

Such a careful, intelligent approach to mission should not be any sort of surprise. And yet John Pritchard, reviewing this book in The Church Times (July 2020), said 'This vision isn't enough'. Ethically speaking, that may be true. But theologically, what more do we want? If the desire for more betrays a longing for a return to an idealised Christian society, then it has missed the point, which is that we still, constantly, misidentify the Church and the Kingdom.

Small minority communities with a missional stance will, Paas assumes, want to be light for the world. However, the vision for how a thoroughly secular society will *benefit* from Christian service and Christian care, reduced in scale and authority, is beyond his scope. How does Christian virtue really spread out from a faithful Christian community? Well, Hauerwas too can be criticised for failing to help us tackle this very question.

Most theology of mission nowadays stresses that it is God who does the saving and the sanctifying, with or without human agency. If we get the spirituality right, (a life of praise and devotion to God), then the rest in a sense is not our problem. This book reflects that belief, impressively, in a way that many church growth programmes seem doomed to neglect.

Edward Cardale, Welwyn

CHEQUE OR CREDIT CARD		DIRECT DEBIT
Individual rate UK:	☐ £22	☐ £20
Institutional rate UK:	☐ £40	☐ £35
Individual international:	☐ £40	
Institutional international:	☐ £50	
Individual copy	☐ £7	

Please complete section 1. Cheque **or** 2. Credit/Debit card **or** 3. Direct debit **(the name and address you give must match the information on your credit/Debit card/bank statement.)**

YOUR DETAILS (Please complete)

Title .... Christian name .... Surname ....

Address: ....

....

....

Postcode .... Daytime telephone no ....

Email: ....

- I enclose a cheque for the total amount of £..............
  payable to Hymns Ancient and Modern Ltd.
- To pay by credit/debit card please visit www.cruciblejournal.co.uk/subscribe
  or contact us on 01603 785911

Instruction to your bank or building society to pay by Direct Debit

Please fill in the whole form using a ball point pen and send to:
Hymns Ancient & Modern Ltd.

Name and full postal address of your bank or building society

To: The Manager

Bank/building society

Address

Postcode

Name(s) of account holder(s)

Bank/building society account number

Branch sort code

Service user number: 2 4 3 2 3 3

Reference

Instruction to your bank or building society
Please pay Hymns Ancient & Modern Ltd Direct Debits from the account detailed in this Instruction subject to the safeguards assured by the Direct Debit Guarantee. I understand that this Instruction may remain with Hymns Ancient & Modern Ltd and, if so, details will be passed electronically to my bank/building society.

Hymns Ancient & Modern Ltd, 13a Hellesdon Park Road, Norwich NR6 5DR

Signature(s)

Banks and building societies may not accept Direct Debit Instructions for some types of account.

This Guarantee should be detached and retained by the payer.

The Direct Debit Guarantee

- This Guarantee is offered by all banks and building societies that accept instructions to pay Direct Debits
- If there are any changes to the amount, date or frequency of your Direct Debit Hymns Ancient & Modern Ltd will notify you 10 working days in advance of your account being debited or as otherwise agreed. If you request Hymns Ancient & Modern Ltd to collect payment, confirmation of the amount and date will be given to you at the time of the request
- If an error is made in the payment of your Direct Debit, by Hymns Ancient & Modern Ltd or your bank or building society, you are entitled to a full and immediate refund of the amount paid from your bank or building society
  - If you receive a refund you are not entitled to, you must pay it back when Hymns Ancient & Modern Ltd asks you to
- You can cancel a Direct Debit at any time by simply contacting your bank or building society. Written confirmation may be required. Please also notify us

www.ingramcontent.com/pod-product-compliance
Lightning Source LLC
Chambersburg PA
CBHW022022290426
44109CB00015B/1276